STAGE MANAGEMENT FORMS & FORMATS

A Collection of Over 100 Forms Ready to Use

Barbara Dilker

DRAMA PUBLISHERS
an imprint of
Quite Specific Media Group Ltd.
New York

(212) 725-5377 v.   (212) 725-8506 f.

web: www.quitespecificmedia.com

email: info@quitespecificmedia.com

Quite Specific Media Group Ltd. imprints:

Costume & Fashion Press

Drama Publishers

By Design Press

Jade Rabbit

EntertainmentPro

To George Anderson,
a man with the courage to take a chance

Contents

CHAPTER 1

Introduction

"Stage Management Forms & Formats," a compilation of forms that can be used by the stage manager in recording and organizing the many lists and plots his job requires, has been created in an attempt to save time and effort during the busy periods of pre-production, rehearsals, and techs.

All forms were designed on 8½-by-11-inch paper and will fit into a standard three-ring notebook. Hopefully many of them will be of use in their present form or will require only slight modification.

REASONS FOR RECORDING PRODUCTION INFORMATION

Some stage managers work with little or no recorded production information. This might be feasible provided nothing happens to the stage manager during the run of the show or life of the company. But accidents do occur and stage managers sometimes leave one show or company for another. It is important, therefore, that assistant stage managers understand a production in its entirety and that all pertinent information is recorded for future reference. If a new stage manager takes over, the transition should be made as smoothly as possible.

It is only fair that assistants and/or replacements have equal access to production information. Anyone who has ever replaced a disorganized stage manager is well aware of the importance of maintaining and passing along production notes.

Saving time and energy is another reason for recording production information. True, this activity also requires a certain amount of time, but when compared with that consumed in tracking down a designer, running to the scene shop, locating the description of an item in the script, etc., he who has organized and recorded his notes comes out the winner.

Another asset for the stage manager is the rapidity with which he can reproduce and disseminate information. Keeping the lines of communication open between departments and individuals is one of his primary tasks.

In a repertory company a production may be shelved for some length of time and later revived. Possibly every member of the company was involved with the original production, but that is highly unlikely. Even if they were, they may have done fifteen productions since then and are unable to remember much about it. Original production information is often used as a base for initiating the revival. Touring companies of previously produced shows often rely heavily on these notes.

REASONS FOR USING FORMS

There is no rule which says that a stage manager must or should use set forms and formats, and very often they cannot or should not be used. Mostly they are a matter of convenience. One advantage of using forms is that recording information can become boring and tiresome. Consequently there is a tendency to get the job done as quickly as possible—even at the expense of doing it inadequately. A form reminds the stage manager what he wants to include or take into consideration when compiling a set of notes. He doesn't have to think about what should be included every time he makes a plot; nor must he consult a production book from a previous show to see how it was done and sit at a typewriter trying to decide how large an area should be relegated to each entry.

Familiarity is also an important element in conserving time. The more something is done consistently, the more efficient the person doing it becomes.

Furthermore, forms tend to require headings, forcing the person using them to keep the information within a given area. Sometimes this can be restricting, but the separation of elements does provide a variety of ways information can be checked, thus freeing the stage manager from dealing with extraneous notes.

A pre-designed form also makes it possible for the stage manager to assign an assistant tasks he might usually do himself. If he knows his form contains requests for information in one certain area, he can be more confident that those items will not be overlooked.

Other advantages of using forms are discussed and illustrated in subsequent chapters.

NOTES ON HOW TO USE FORMS

Since one major consideration in designing these forms was to make them as flexible as possible, there are places where headings have not been specified. The stage manager should indicate these when using the form.

Some forms include dashes along the margin to aid in drawing division lines. Other forms are partially lined to provide a variety of separation points. A few include large open areas with no dashes or lines; this has been done to permit totally unrestricted division of the area.

Most forms contain a notation "Page_____of_____" in the upper right hand corner. The first blank is for recording the page number of that particular sheet; the second is to indicate the total number of sheets used. For instance, the second page of a five page plot would read, "Page__2__of__5__."

At the bottom of some forms there is a "Key" entry. This area should be used to record and define abbreviations and symbols used on that page. Although standard stage directions and abbreviations need not be entered, personal or unfamiliar abbreviations should be.

CHAPTER 2

Audition & Casting Forms

The role the stage manager plays in the interview/audition period of a play will vary from one production to another. Sometimes the stage manager is not hired until the show has been completely cast; at other times he is expected to handle the scheduling of auditions and interviews, read with the actors who are auditioning, etc.

This chapter includes samples of forms the stage manager can use when he is involved with the casting of a show.

INTERVIEW/AUDITION SCHEDULE (Form 2-A)

When the audition or interview is being held for a pre-arranged number of people (i.e., an agent's call, call backs, etc.), a schedule should be worked out including the time of the interview or audition and the name of the actor who has the appointment; the role or position the person is being considered for; name, address, and telephone number of his agency and agent; and contact information.

The following examples illustrate several ways in which Form 2-A can be used to record audition or interview schedules:

TIME	NAME	ROLE CONSIDERED FOR	NOTES
10 AM	Linda Davis	Margaret Hero (US)	Home: 531-2983 Service: KI2-7000

TIME	NAME	AGENT	NOTES
11 AM	David Johnson	Hollywood Mgmt. (Sam Kline) 785-9202	Agent not handling this call.

KEY: (US)—Understudy

AUDITION FORMS (Forms 2-B & 2-C)

It is standard procedure for each actor to complete an audition form or card when he arrives, thus ensuring that the company has complete information for everyone auditioning. Set forms are useful

3

because they establish a specific physical place where information can be found, making it easier for the stage manager to check that everything is complete.

This information can either be entered on a piece of paper, index card, or both. It is advisable to have these forms completed in duplicate, since one will become a working copy and the other will serve as a safety. Stapling one copy to the photo and resume and filing the second copy enables the director to take the photo, resume, and form with him while the stage manager retains the second copy—or vice versa.

Forms 2–B and 2–C are examples of two formats that can be used for audition forms. This information can also be printed on three-by-five-inch or five-by-seven-inch cards, which can be reproduced and distributed at the audition. If the stage manager does not have time to get them printed, he can post a sample copy on the call board and request that the actors follow that format in filling out their cards or forms. Form 2–B was designed for Equity actors; and Form 2–C for non-union performers.

INFORMATION IN PLACE OF RESUME (Form 2–D)

Most professional actors will have a printed copy of their resume which they usually attach to their photo; many non-professionals will not. In any event, there are some circumstances when any actor may be caught without a resume. The stage manager can save time for the director by making sure each actor has a copy of his resume. If this is not the case, the stage manager should see that the actor makes a listing of his experience before starting the audition or interview.

Since actors are usually nervous at auditions and interviews, it may be difficult for them to remember the information included on their resumes. A format similar to Form 2–D can be designed to aid the actor in recording his credits.

PRODUCTION FACT SHEETS (Forms 2–E & 2–F)

A production fact sheet is simply a listing of basic information pertaining to the production. This sheet has its major use before and during auditions and in the early part of the rehearsal period. A copy should be posted on the call board for all interview and audition calls. When the show has finally been cast, it is a good idea to provide each member of the company with a copy.

The information recorded on this sheet will vary depending on the type of company, the play(s) being presented, the personnel, and the schedules. A format similar to Form 2–E might be used for a company producing a single musical, whereas Form 2–F has been designed for use in repertory companies.

CHARACTER DESCRIPTION & AUDITION SCENES (Form 2–G)

When an actor arrives at an audition, he wants to know first what roles are available. Then he will want to look over the scenes he will be asked to read. The stage manager will not have time to describe every character for each actor; it is advisable, therefore, to post information regarding character description and audition scenes and refer actors to the call board.

A format similar to the one on Form 2–G might be used to record character descriptions and audition scenes. The form is self-explanatory, but a word about the "Notes" heading. This area might be used to indicate the availability of the role (i.e., "Cast, Understudy Open"); understudy roles that the actor might be expected to assume (i.e., "Understudy to Romeo"); or more specific requirements set by the director (i.e., "Authentic British Accent").

SELECTED READINGS (Form 2–H)

By the time the audition stage of production has been reached, the director and stage manager should be thoroughly familiar with the character descriptions. Now the information they will need deals with the readings that have been chosen.

A list of readings should clearly indicate which character or characters use that particular scene, the act and scene of the selection, the script pages where it can be located, and any notes that could be valuable to the stage manager or director. These notes might consist of additional characters the stage manager would be expected to "read in," or some identification of the selection, such as "Tea Scene" or "Confrontation." A format similar to Form 2–H can be used to record this information.

RECORD OF AUDITION SCRIPTS (Form 2-I)

Since usually it is neither possible nor practical to have a script for every actor auditioning, it is important to keep track of where each copy is going. Generally actors return them before leaving an audition, but there are exceptions: an actor may be permitted to keep the script until the next audition, or a copy may be sent to an agent.

In any event, it is wise to have everyone using a script leave his name, telephone, and number of the script being used. When the script is returned, the actor's name can simply be crossed out. This safeguards against permanent loss of a script should an actor accidentally slip it into his bag and take it home. When someone is permitted to keep a script, it is wise to record the date it should be returned.

A format such as that illustrated on Form 2-I can be used to handle the assignment of audition scripts.

CASTING ASSIGNMENTS (Forms 2-J, 2-K, & 2-L)

Casting assignment sheets can and should evolve into cast lists. These lists should be started as soon as the first role has been cast and subsequent additions made as casting progresses. Some companies may have understudies, alternates, and standbys; other companies may make no provisions for these positions.

Examples of possible formats for single production casting assignments are illustrated on Forms 2-J and 2-K. It is advisable to list all of the character names and enter the actor's name when the role is cast.

When working with a repertory company it is often necessary to know what roles an actor will be playing or understudying for the duration of the season. Because of the inconvenience of consulting a separate cast list for each production, it is advisable to design a grid organizing the needed information and listing the entries alphabetically by the actors' last names.

The stage manager may wish to keep separate charts of the roles and the understudy assignments, etc. If, however, he decides to record all the information on one sheet, it is important that each position be clearly marked. It may be wise to work out a series of abbreviations for this purpose such as, ALT—Alternate, SB—Standby, US—Understudy. In addition, the stage manager might use a felt tip highlighter pen to make the assigned roles stand out.

The following is an example of Form 2-L utilized for a repertory company, with all assignments listed on one sheet:

ACTOR'S NAME	OTHELLO	MUCH ADO	HAMLET	RICHARD III
L. Kayle	Roderigo	Conrad	Laertes	---
	Iago ALT	Don Pedro US	---	Richard SB

UNDERSTUDY ASSIGNMENTS & CHANGES (Form 2-M)

Inadequate understudy coverage is usually a result of not thinking through all cast changes that must be made every time an actor is out. The purpose of maintaining an understudy change plot is to guarantee that all roles are adequately covered and to help anticipate problems arising when an understudy performs.

"Internal covers" can create a domino effect continuing until one of the following occurs: an actor is able to do both his own role and the understudy assignment in the same performance; a role can be cut or consolidated; a general understudy or standby can take over or, you discover there is no way of covering the role with the present casting.

The following cast list illustrates how Form 2-M can be used to record understudy changes. In this example the coverage is adequate:

ROLE	ACTOR	UNDERSTUDY
Penelope	Sue Clark	Joan Blackwell
Stevens	Johnny Jackson	Sean O'Connor
Horace	Sean O'Connor	Johnny Jackson
Janie	Joan Blackwell	Andrea Lynn

ROLE	UNDERSTUDY	CHANGE
Penelope	Joan Blackwell	Janie —— Andrea Lynn
Stevens	Sean O'Connor	Plays both Stevens and Horace
Horace	Johnny Jackson	Plays both Stevens and Horace
Janie	Andrea Lynn	

FORM 2–A

INTERVIEW/AUDITION SCHEDULE

Date_____

PRODUCTION_____

Page_____ of_____

TIME	NAME		NOTES

FORM 2–B

Date _____

AUDITION FORM

COMPANY OR PRODUCTION _____,_____

INTERVIEW _____ AUDITION _____ CALL BACK _____

NAME _____ AGENCY _____

ADDRESS _____ AGENT _____

PHONE # _____ ADDRESS _____

SERVICE # _____ PHONE # _____

IS AGENT HANDLING THIS CALL? _____   ARE YOU SIGNED WITH AGENT? _____

UNION AFFILIATION:

AEA _____   AGVA _____   AGMA _____   AFTRA _____   SAG _____   OTHER

HEIGHT _____   WEIGHT _____   HAIR _____   EYES _____

PLAYABLE AGE RANGE _____

VOCAL QUALITY _____   VOCAL RANGE _____

SING _____ DANCE _____ PLAY INSTRUMENT _____ ACCENTS _____

FENCE _____   OTHER SPECIALTIES (Specify) _____

Please notify us if you have a change of address, phone number or agent.

_____

(Please Do Not Write Below This Line)

NOTES:

BY _____

FORM 2–C

<u>PLEASE PRINT</u>   Date _____

<u>AUDITION FORM</u>

COMPANY OR PRODUCTION _____

INTERVIEW _____ AUDITION _____ CALL BACK _____

NAME: _____

ADDRESS: _____

_____

PHONE: _____

HEIGHT _____ WEIGHT _____ HAIR _____ EYES _____

PLAYABLE AGE RANGE _____

DO YOU PLAY AN INSTRUMENT (SPECIFY) _____

SPECIAL SKILLS (SPECIFY) _____

_____

STAGE EXPERIENCE:

TV OR FILM EXPERIENCE:

EDUCATION AND TRAINING:

REFERENCES:

_____

(PLEASE DO NOT WRITE BELOW THIS LINE)

BY _____

FORM 2–D

<u>PLEASE PRINT</u>   Date _____

INFORMATION IN PLACE OF RESUME

PROFESSIONAL EXPERIENCE:
(Under a union contract)

NON-PROFESSIONAL EXPERIENCE:

EDUCATION & TRAINING:

FOREIGN LANGUAGES (Specify):

ACCENTS (Specify):

SPECIALTIES:

REFERENCES:

FORM 2–E

PRODUCTION FACT SHEET

Date _____   Page ____ of ____

PRODUCTION _____

NAME OF COMPANY _____

TYPE OF CONTRACT _____ CATEGORY _____

TYPE OF PLAY _____ SCRIPTS AVAILABLE FROM _____

BRIEF NOTES ABOUT PLAY _____

_____

_____

_____

_____

DATES & PLACES

  REHEARSALS _____

_____

  OUT-OF-TOWN TRYOUTS _____

_____

_____

  TOUR _____

_____

_____

_____

  PREVIEWS _____

  OPENING _____

  CLOSING _____

PRODUCERS _____

GENERAL MANAGERS _____

DIRECTOR _____

CHOREOGRAPHER _____

PLAYWRIGHT _____

COMPOSER _____

LYRICIST _____

MUSICAL DIRECTOR _____

CASTING COORDINATOR _____

PRODUCTION STAGE MANAGER _____

DESIGNERS: SCENIC _____

             COSTUME _____

             LIGHTING _____

FORM 2–F

PRODUCTION FACT SHEET

NAME OF COMPANY _____

TYPE OF CONTRACT _____ CATEGORY _____ DATES OF SEASON: FROM _____ TO _____

ARTISTIC DIRECTOR _____ MANAGING DIRECTOR _____

TITLE OF PLAY			
PLAYWRIGHT			
TYPE OF PLAY			
DIRECTOR			
REHEARSALS			
OPENING			
CLOSING			
SCENIC DESIGNER			
COSTUME DESIGNER			
LIGHTING DESIGNER			
SCRIPTS AVAILABLE FROM			
NOTES			

FORM 2–G

CHARACTER DESCRIPTION & AUDITION SCENES

PRODUCTION _____

CHARACTER	DESCRIPTION	AUDITION SCENES	NOTES

FORM 2–H

SELECTED READINGS

Date _____   Page ____ of ____

PRODUCTION _____

CHARACTER	ACT & SCENE	PAGES	NOTES

FORM 2–I

RECORD OF AUDITION SCRIPTS

Date _____   Page ____ of ____

PRODUCTION _____

#	ASSIGNED TO	DATE TO BE RETURNED	PHONE #'S

FORM 2–J

<u>CAST LIST</u>

Date _____   Page ____ of ____

PRODUCTION _____

CHARACTER	ACTOR PLAYING ROLE	UNDERSTUDY

FORM 2–K

CASTING ASSIGNMENTS

PRODUCTION _____

CHARACTER	ACTOR	ALTERNATIVES	UNDERSTUDIES	NOTES

FORM 2–L

CASTING ASSIGNMENTS

ACTOR'S NAME	COMPANY _____

KEY:

FORM 2–M

UNDERSTUDY ASSIGNMENTS & CHANGES

PRODUCTION _____

ROLE	UNDERSTUDY	CHANGE

CHAPTER 3

Check Lists & Note Forms

GRID CHECK LIST (Form 3-A)

A simple attendance check list can be made from Form 3-A by entering names and phone numbers of the actors or company members in the left hand column and dates at the top of the remaining columns. Including phone numbers on the check list will save the stage manager time and effort in looking it up on the contact sheet. This type of check list might also be used for collecting information, such as bios, insurance cards, choice of hotels, etc., and for calling actors about changes in rehearsal schedules.

It is a good idea for the stage manager to keep one copy of the check list on his clip board during rehearsals and another by his home phone. These lists are also useful to other staff members in the company. The stage manager should see that assistant stage managers, production assistants, and other people helping out during the rehearsal period have their own copies, and the administrative office is usually grateful for a small supply.

This format is also useful as an inventory check list for the technical departments of touring companies. Instead of listing names in the left hand column, a description of each item to be checked is entered. These lists can easily be stapled onto road boxes for use during strikes and load outs to insure that nothing has been accidentally left behind.

The ways in which this form can be used are endless.

ITEMIZED CHECK LIST (Form 3-B)

This format is particularly helpful for compiling frequently used itemized lists such as supplies the stage manager wants to include in his kit; items that should be checked when obtaining a new rehearsal hall; tasks that should be performed when joining a new company; or basic stationery supplies that should be acquired before rehearsals start. This list, too, can be used in a number of ways.

GENERAL NOTE FORMS (Forms 3-C & 3-D)

The stage manager may wish to have forms similar to 3-C and 3-D printed, or he can simply reproduce them on a lined yellow pad as needed. Most printers who do offset work can bind these forms into pads.

It is important that this form be extremely flexible since the stage manager never knows from one moment to the next what notes he will be taking or how much writing space will be needed.

When a lined sheet is used, it is only necessary to make vertical divisions to create definite areas for recording notes.. The headings for each area can be set off by making the lines above and below the heading bolder and/or by drawing over the heading with a felt tip highlighter pen. The entire sheet of paper need not be divided at once; additional areas can be defined and headings added as needed.

A partial example of Form 3-C illustrates how this format may be used:

TO BE DONE	SOUND	PROPS
Get another table	Sleigh bells	Tea tray
Revise scene breakdown	(45 sec.)	Sugar bowl
Set up meeting with John		Creamer
Get bios to Margie		Tea pot
Check on progress of pouf		Sugar shell
		2 Teacups
		2 Saucers
COSTUMES	LIGHTS	
Add pockets/Elmer's coat	6:00 Cue Lite	
Jane's 2nd change/30 seconds		

REMINDER SHEET (Form 3-E)

One of the main purposes of the reminder sheet is to record notes that cannot or should not be taken care of immediately. For instance, if the stage manager is supposed to check on the arrival of a wig but knows it is not scheduled to arrive until a certain date, rewriting the note everyday until it does arrive would be a waste of time. He can simply enter the date it is expected to arrive and the note "check wig" on his reminder sheet. Similarly, if the director tells the stage manager, "Remind me to have a run-thru next Friday," the stage manager should record it on his reminder sheet.

Just as the stage manager checks his notes and report sheets daily, he should also make it a habit to check the reminder sheet. By doing this he can make new entries on the reminder sheet from his notes and report sheets and transfer information from the reminder sheet to his notes for the following day. Creating a column which can be checked when the item has been taken care of eliminates the need to constantly reread notes about already completed jobs.

A format similar to the one for Form 3-E can be used in making a reminder sheet.

SIGN-IN SHEETS (Forms 3-F & 3-G)

The format for sign-in sheets may vary from one company or production to another. A separate sign-in sheet for each performance might simply list the actor's name followed by a space or line, as follows:

John Ashley_____Connie West _____
Cynthia Butler_____Larry Yost _____

Some stage managers prefer to use only one sign-in sheet per week. This has the advantage of requiring fewer sheets and having to change them less often, but in using it the stage manager runs the risk of company members signing in far in advance of the call and then reporting five minutes before curtain time, or of someone accidentally signing in on the wrong line. Form 3-F will serve as a weekly sign-in sheet by entering the names in the first column and the days and dates at the top of the remaining columns.

On a tour the company will constantly be using unfamiliar facilities requiring the stage manager to assign new dressing rooms, wardrobe rooms, etc., for each engagement. It is helpful if the company can find their new dressing room assignments and the location of other facilities on the sign-in sheet. This also cuts down on the amount of paper the stage manager has to carry in his road box.

Form 3-G is a sample format that can be used as a daily sign-in sheet for a touring company.

FORM 3–A

CHECK LIST

PRODUCTION _____

FORM 3–B

<u>   </u> CHECK LIST

Date <u>   </u>   Page <u>   </u> of <u>   </u>

        PRODUCTION <u>   </u>

☐ _____   ☐ _____

☐ _____   ☐ _____

☐ _____   ☐ _____

☐ _____   ☐ _____

☐ _____   ☐ _____

☐ _____   ☐ _____

☐ _____   ☐ _____

☐ _____   ☐ _____

☐ _____   ☐ _____

☐ _____   ☐ _____

☐ _____   ☐ _____

☐ _____   ☐ _____

☐ _____   ☐ _____

☐ _____   ☐ _____

☐ _____   ☐ _____

☐ _____   ☐ _____

☐ _____   ☐ _____

☐ _____   ☐ _____

☐ _____   ☐ _____

☐ _____   ☐ _____

☐ _____   ☐ _____

☐ _____   ☐ _____

☐ _____   ☐ _____

☐ _____   ☐ _____

☐ _____   ☐ _____

FORM 3-C

FORM 3–D

FORM 3–E

REMINDER SHEET

_____   Page ____ of ____

PRODUCTION _____

DONE	DATE	REMINDER

FORM 3-F

SIGN-IN SHEET

PRODUCTION _____

WEEK OF _____   HALF HOUR CALLS:

NOTES:

FORM 3-G

SIGN-IN SHEET

PRODUCTION _____

DATE _____   HALF HOUR _____

CITY & STATE _____   THEATRE _____

NAME	SIGN-IN	FLOOR	ROOM	GENERAL INFORMATION
				WARDROBE:
				MAKEUP:
				HAIR:
				GREENROOM:
				TELEPHONE:
				STAGE MANAGERS:
				COMPANY MANAGER:
				LADIES' ROOM:
				MEN'S ROOM:
				OTHER:

CHAPTER 4

Report Sheets & Performance Logs

REHEARSAL REPORT SHEETS (Form 4–A & 4–B)

There are two major reasons for completing rehearsal reports. First, they provide the stage manager with a format for recording rehearsal times, rehearsal progress, technical changes, etc. Second, since the producer or artistic director cannot attend every rehearsal, they provide him with a daily report of what is happening in rehearsals and what new developments are taking place.

The rehearsal report sheet should include the number of the rehearsal; name of the production; day and date of rehearsal; if rehearsal started late, an explanation of why it was detained; and the names of any personnel reporting late. It should also contain a record of rehearsal time, running time of any full acts or scenes, and a brief notation describing what was rehearsed that day. Form 4–B relegates the remaining space to specific technical departments and miscellaneous notes such as accidents, publicity notes, actors excused or absent from rehearsal, etc. Since most of the notes taken during the rehearsal period deal with technical elements, this format makes it easier to separate notes, write memos, and check on progress. Form 4–C provides no departmental separation for technical notes. The additional space is used for notes pertaining to attendance, injuries, notices, etc.

These reports are extremely helpful if the stage manager has to leave an assistant in charge of a rehearsal. It is advisable that the stage manager review these reports at least once a week to double check that he has taken care of all items mentioned.

PERFORMANCE REPORT SHEETS (Forms 4–C & 4–D)

In contrast to rehearsal reports, performance reports record a show's running time and total time elapsed. Running time is the actual time it took to perform the show without intermissions, and total time elapsed includes the time consumed by intermissions.

Since directors rarely stay for the entire run of a production, they may request that copies of these reports be forwarded to them or that they receive progress reports every so often. These reports can provide a basis for correspondence with the director.

TOURING REPORT SHEET (Form 4–E)

The front side of the touring report sheet is basically the same format as the performance report, except that it contains information pertaining to the specific engagement: city and state, theatre, and scheduled curtain time. The curtain times for a stationary production usually adhere to a set weekly schedule, but on the road there may be a large variation in times. In this book a variation of Form 4–A has been used on the front, but Form 4–B with the above changes can be substituted if desired.

The back of this form deals with rehearsals and other events that might have occurred on that day;

time records of set ups, strikes, etc.; and information about the theatre where the company is performing. With the exception of "Rehearsal/Other Events" and "Time Record," it is usually necessary to complete this information only once per engagement. Rehearsal information should be entered whenever there is a scheduled rehearsal, and a time record should be kept for each changeover if the company is performing more than one show.

Information pertaining to the physical facilities, local contacts and crews can be valuable in planning future tours for the company. A copy of the second side of this report should be stapled to the theatre information questionnaire (See Form 12–D) and filed in the production office when the company returns to home base. It is also a good idea for the stage manager to keep a copy of this information for his own files.

SCENE BY SCENE REHEARSAL RECORD (Form 4–F)

When a show consists of many different scenes, it is often helpful for the stage manager and the director to have a record of how much rehearsal time was spent on each scene and how much time has elapsed since it was last rehearsed. Because this information changes every day it is a good idea to record it in very light pencil, use an overlay of tissue paper, or set it up on a miniature blackboard.

An example of the use of Form 4–F is illustrated below:

ACT & SCENE	PAGES	DATE LAST REHEARSED	LENGTH OF TIME	TOTAL TO DATE	NOTES
I, 1	15—42	6/1/80	1½ hrs.	12 hrs.	
I, 2	42—50	5/25/80	½ hr.	3 hrs.	Schedule 1 hr. tomorrow

PERFORMANCE LOGS (Forms 4–G & 4–H)

A performance log is a record of the running time and total time elapsed for each performance. This information is usually recorded by acts or by scenes. Its purpose is to compare the running time of each performance to that of previous performances.

When a show starts running longer each evening it is usually an indication that something is going wrong—the actors may be running out of energy, becoming bored with the show, making minor changes in business or characterizations, etc. Once the stage manager is aware of a lack of consistency in running times, he should begin looking for the reason. If the differences in timings indicate a change in quality of the performance, the stage manager should take whatever steps are necessary to correct the situation.

Form 4–G has been designed to accommodate the performance times for a one, two, or three act play. An example of how this form might be utilized follows:

DAY & DATE Saturday, August 8, 1982

CITY & STATE Santa Monica, California

ACT I UP 9:06

                        43 min.

ACT I DOWN 9:49

  INTERMISSION 11 min.

ACT II UP 10:00

                        44 min.

ACT II DOWN 10:44

  INTERMISSION 11 min.

ACT III UP 10:55

                        27 min.

ACT III DOWN 11:22

RUNNING TIME 1 hr., 54 min.

TOTAL TIME 2 hrs., 16 min.

Form 4–H has been designed to accommodate a variable number of acts and scenes. The information from the above example transferred to this form might appear as follows:

DAY & DATE CITY & STATE	ACT & SCENE	UP	DOWN	TOTAL	INTER	RUNNING	TOTAL
Sat., 8/8/82	I	9:06	9:49	43 min.	11 min.		
Santa Monica,	II	10:00	10:44	44 min.	11 min.		
California	III	10:55	11:22	27 min.		1:54	2:16

FORM 4–A

<u>REHEARSAL REPORT SHEET</u>

Rehearsal # _____ of _____

Date _____ Morn ____ After ____ Eve ____

Rehearsal Detained By _____

Personnel Reporting Late _____

_____

_____

Stage Manager

Reh.								
Break								

Run Thru: ACT I _____ ACT II _____ ACT III _____ ACT IV _____ ACT V _____

Rehearsal

Scenery

Lights	Sound

Costumes

Props

Miscellaneous

FORM 4–B

<u>REHEARSAL REPORT SHEET</u>

Rehearsal # _____ of _____

Date _____ Morn ____ After ____ Eve ____

Rehearsal Detained By _____

_____

_____
Stage Manager

Reh.								
Break								

Run Thru: ACT I _____   ACT II _____   ACT III _____   ACT IV _____   ACT V _____

Rehearsal	
Late	**Absent/Excused**
Accidents/Injuries	**Notices: Given/Received**
Technical Notes	

FORM 4–C

PERFORMANCE REPORT SHEET

Performance # _____ of _____

Date _____ Morn ____ After ____ Eve ____

Curtain Detained By _____

Personnel Reporting Late _____

_____

_____
Stage Manager

	I	Int.	II	Int.	III	TOTALS	
Up							Inter.
Down							Playing
Total							Total

Performance

Scenery

Lights | **Sound**

Costumes

Props

Miscellaneous

FORM 4–D

PERFORMANCE REPORT SHEET

Performance # _____ of _____
Date _____ Morn ____ After ____ Eve ____
Curtain Detained By _____
_____

Stage Manager

	I	Int.	II	Int.	III	TOTALS	
Up							Inter.
Down							Playing
Total							Total

Performance	
Late	Replacements/Understudies
Accidents/Injuries	Notices: Given/Received
Technical Notes	

FORM 4–E

TOURING REPORT SHEET

Performance # _____ of _____
Day & Date _____
Scheduled Curtain Time
Curtain Detained By _____
Personnel Reporting Late _____
_____

_____
Stage Manager

CITY & STATE _____ THEATRE _____

	I	Int.	II	Int.	III	TOTALS	
Up							Inter.
Down							Playing
Total							Total

Performance

Scenery

Lights	Sound

Costumes

Props

Miscellaneous

FORM 4–E (Side Two)

ENGAGEMENT & THEATRE NOTES

Time Record	Rehearsal/Other Events
Crew Arrival _____ Load In Started _____ Set Up Completed _____ Company Arrival _____ Length of Strike_____ Load Out Completed _____	

Local Contacts

Loading Area

Stage & Wing Area

House Lighting Equipment	House Sound Equipment

Local Crew Info

Dressing & Rest Room Facilities

Additional Notes

FORM 4–F

PRODUCTION _____

SCENE BY SCENE REHEARSAL RECORD

ACT & SCENE	PAGES	DATE LAST REHEARSED	LENGTH OF TIME	TOTAL TO DATE	NOTES

FORM 4–G

PERFORMANCE LOG

DATES_____PRODUCTION_____

DAY & DATE_____   DAY & DATE_____

CITY & STATE_____   CITY & STATE_____

ACT I UP _____   ACT I UP _____

ACT I DOWN _____ _____   ACT I DOWN _____ _____

   INTERMISSION _____   INTERMISSION _____

ACT II UP_____   ACT II UP_____

ACT II DOWN _____ _____   ACT II DOWN _____ _____

   INTERMISSION _____   INTERMISSION _____

ACT III UP _____   ACT III UP _____

ACT III DOWN _____ _____   ACT III DOWN _____ _____

RUNNING TIME_____   RUNNING TIME_____

TOTAL TIME _____   TOTAL TIME _____

DAY & DATE_____   DAY & DATE_____

CITY & STATE_____   CITY & STATE_____

ACT I UP _____   ACT I UP _____

ACT I DOWN _____ _____   ACT I DOWN _____ _____

   INTERMISSION _____   INTERMISSION _____

ACT II UP_____   ACT II UP_____

ACT II DOWN _____ _____   ACT II DOWN _____ _____

   INTERMISSION _____   INTERMISSION _____

ACT III UP _____   ACT III UP _____

ACT III DOWN _____ _____   ACT III DOWN·_____ _____

RUNNING TIME_____   RUNNING TIME_____

TOTAL TIME _____   TOTAL TIME _____

DAY & DATE_____   DAY & DATE_____

CITY & STATE_____   CITY & STATE_____

ACT I UP _____   ACT I UP _____

ACT I DOWN _____ _____   ACT I DOWN _____ _____

   INTERMISSION _____   INTERMISSION _____

ACT II UP_____   ACT II UP_____

ACT II DOWN _____ _____   ACT II DOWN _____ _____

   INTERMISSION _____   INTERMISSION _____

ACT III UP _____   ACT III UP _____

ACT III DOWN _____ _____   ACT III DOWN_____ _____

RUNNING TIME_____   RUNNING TIME_____

TOTAL TIME _____   TOTAL TIME _____

FORM 4–H

PERFORMANCE LOG

Dates_____   Page_____ of____

PRODUCTION_____

DAY & DATE CITY & STATE	ACT & SCENE	UP	DOWN	TOTAL	INTER	RUNNING	TOTAL

Stage
Management
Forms & Formats

CHAPTER 5

Schedules & Time Sheets

Scheduling is one of the stage manager's most important duties. Every production requires some kind of overall schedule for the entire rehearsal period or season as well as daily rehearsal schedules listing the calls for each day. During the rehearsal period there are also photo calls, costume fittings, production meetings, designer's conferences, publicity engagements, etc., to be scheduled into or around the rehearsal time.

In this chapter schedules can be used in any type of company; others have been designed for specific types.

SCHEDULING CALENDAR (Form 5-A)

Form 5-A is set up as a calendar format and can be used for overall planning on any production or season. The small square in the upper left-hand corner of each box is for the date.

The following is a partial listing of some information the stage manager may want to enter on this type of schedule:

Rehearsals—Starting date, date actors should be "off book," total number of rehearsal hours available on each day, starting date of techs, etc.

Technical—Design conferences, final design approval, starting date of construction, progress visits to the shops, dress parade, load-in, etc.

Publicity—Photo calls, interviews, guest appearances, etc.

Touring—Travel information, engagement and performance information, arrival and load-in times, etc.

Repertory—Information about which show is playing, which shows are rehearsing, performance times, etc.

If the schedule is extremely heavy or complicated it is often helpful to use a color code for recording the entries. For instance, three different colors may be chosen to create a separation of rehearsal plans, tech entries, and publicity engagements. In a repertory company each show may be assigned a specific color; this helps the stage manager to spot quickly all entries pertaining to a single production.

Frequently, multiple entries will have to be made on one day. A separation can be achieved by dividing the box representing the day vertically, horizontally, or diagonally.

The following is a partial example of Form 5-A with sample entries:

MONDAY	TUESDAY	WEDNESDAY	THURSDAY

1   5:00 PM
 	
Prod. meeting/
Greenroom
	2 10:00 AM
	
	1st rehearsal/
	Main stage
		3 10:00 AM
		
		Company photo/
		Garden
		
		6:30 PM -- Dir.
		   interview/
		   Greenroom
			4
			
			DAY OFF

This form should be used for brief entries of a general nature. Another format should be used for expanded or detailed schedules.

PRODUCTION TIMETABLE (Form 5-B)

A production timetable is simply a calendar, list, or chart of dates and deadlines for all technical departments. Its purpose is to present an overall, concise picture of all technical scheduling.

The layout of Form 5-B facilitates checking the timetable for all departments on each day or one department for the entire production period. The following is an abbreviated example of a production timetable:

DATE	COSTUMES	LIGHTS	PROPS	SCENERY	SOUND
9/15		Load-in/hang		Load-in/set-up	Load-in/set-up
9/16	Load-in/set-up	Hang/focus	Load-in/set-up	Set-up	Set-up
9/17	Dress parade	Set levels/ pre-tech	Pre-tech	Pre-tech	Set levels/ pre-tech

REHEARSAL TIME ALLOTMENT (Form 5-C)

Form 5-C's primary use is for companies that rehearse more than one production each day. One of the most difficult tasks in stage managing a repertory or multiple-production company is the division of rehearsal time blocks between productions and directors. Before rehearsals begin it is a good idea for the stage manager to have a rough idea of how the major block of rehearsal time each day should be assigned to insure that each show is allotted sufficient rehearsal time. Adjustments will probably have to be made as the rehearsal period progresses, but at all times the stage manager should try to maintain a fair balance between the productions.

Form 5-C can be used to work out the division of available rehearsal time. It also shows at a glance where each show stands in total rehearsal hours for the week. An example of the use of Form 5-C follows:

DAY & DATE	KING LEAR	TWELFTH NIGHT	RICHARD III	HAMLET
Mon., 6/8/82	DARK	DARK	OFF	OFF
Tues., 6/9/82	3-3/4 P	DARK	2½	2
Wed., 6/10/82	DARK	2½ P	2½	3

KEY: P--Performance

The above format can also be applied to rehearsals of musicals if it is necessary to work out divisions of time between the director, choreographer, and musical director.

DAILY REHEARSAL SCHEDULES (Forms 5-D & 5-E)

For all productions it is necessary to work out a specific schedule for each day's rehearsal. Regardless of the format used, the schedule should include the following information: name of the production being rehearsed; day, date, and time of rehearsal; place of rehearsal; description of what is to be rehearsed; and the people involved in that rehearsal.

A single production rehearsing in one place might have a schedule like the following:

Monday, June 1, 1979

A Midsummer Night's Dream   Rehearsal Hall

10:00 AM—I, 1—Theseus, Hippolyta, Philostrate, Egeus, Hermia, Lysander, Demetrius, Helena, Court Attendants

11:30 AM—IV,1—Add Bottom, Fairy, Puck, Oberon, Titania, Peaseblossom, Cobweb, Moth, Mustardseed, Oberon's Train, Titania's Train

  1:30 PM—LUNCH BREAK

A single production rehearsing in two different places might have a schedule like the following:

TIME	REHEARSAL HALL	DANCE STUDIO
10:00 AM	IV,2 -- Quince, Snug, Bottom, Flute, Snout, Starveling	II,2 Dance -- Titania, Fairy, Peaseblossom, Cobweb, Moth, Mustardseed
11:30 AM	III,1 -- Same	V,2 Second Dance -- Add Puck, Oberon, Oberon's Train, Titania's Train
NOTE:	All members of the Fairy Kingdom bring dance rehearsal costumes with them.	

When the rehearsal schedule contains the calls for more than one production, it is advisable to enter the name of the company as well as the name of each production. A rehearsal schedule for multiple productions rehearsing in two different locations might appear as follows:

TIME	A MIDSUMMER NIGHT'S DREAM Main Stage	ROMEO & JULIET Rehearsal Studio
10:00 AM	III,2 -- Hermia, Lysander, Demetrius, Helena, Puck, Oberon	II,1 -- Benvolio, Mercutio, Romeo

Items such as costume fittings, photo calls, and notes may be added to these forms by designating another column for that purpose at the bottom of the schedule, or by making a notation to "See Photo Call," etc. as a cross reference to another sheet or schedule.

Form 5-D can be used as a vertical layout of any of the above formats, whereas Form 5-E is merely a horizontal layout of the same format.

PHOTO CALL (Form 5-F)

When a photographer takes candid pictures during a dress rehearsal, there is usually no need to indicate what shots should be taken; he will simply take random shots that he finds interesting. If the director wants specific shots, the stage manager can simply give a list of them to the photographer in advance of the rehearsal.

When a photo call is scheduled for the purpose of taking specific shots, it will go a lot smoother if everyone is well informed as to where and when the session is scheduled, what poses will be taken, who is involved in each shot, and the order in which they will be taken.

The stage manager should get as much information as possible regarding the call recorded and distributed well in advance of the session. This allows time for the photographer, actors, and technicians to familiarize themselves with the schedule and to make the necessary preparations.

An example of Form 5–F might appear as follows:

#	ACT & SCENE	DESCRIPTION	ACTORS INVOLVED
1	I,1	Sword fight TYBALT: "What, drawn and talk of peace? I hate the word as I hate hell, all Montagues, and thee. Have at thee, coward!"	(L to R) George Willis (Tybalt) Fred Jones (Benvolio)

BOOKING SCHEDULE & FACT SHEET (Form 5–G)

The purpose of this form is to help the stage manager record scheduling information for each touring engagement. The following information should be recorded for each engagement:

1. City and state of the booking
2. Dates the company will be in residence
3. Local group which is sponsoring the company
4. Contact information for persons in charge of the theatre and the sponsoring organization
5. Name, address, and phone numbers of the theatre where the company will be performing
6. Name, address, and phone number of the hotel where the company will be staying
7. Type of stage (i.e., arena, proscenium, etc.)
8. Indication of whether the theatre has an agreement with IATSE, the stagehands' union
9. Performance information for that engagement
10. Other events that will take place (i.e., lectures, interviews, etc.)
11. Travel information for the next engagement

On Form 5–G the "Performance" section has been designed to accommodate a touring repertory company. If only one show is touring, the "Show" heading can be eliminated. Usually the "Load-In/Set-Up" and the "Strike/Load-Out" are consecutive. When these tasks are not consecutive, separate entries should be made for each on the appropriate date and marked to indicate the task to be performed.

The following is an example of completed performance information in which strike occurs immediately after a performance, but load-out does not start until the next morning:

#	DAY & DATE	PERF. TIME	SHOW	LOAD IN SET UP	STRIKE LOAD OUT	NOTES
13	Thurs. 6/4/82	8:00 PM	Moon	9:00 AM	None	4 PM brushup rehearsal
14	Fri. 6/5/82	8:00 PM	Moon	None	11:00 PM	
22	Sat. 6/6/82	8:00 PM	Othello	9:00 AM	11:30 PM strike	
--	Sun. 6/7/82	No. perf	Othello	None	9:00 AM load-out	Travel to Pittsburgh, PA

In addition to the major productions, many touring companies schedule other events and appointments. These often include classroom demonstrations, lectures, and interviews with local newspapers and TV stations. Information pertaining to these items can be entered under the "Special Events" section. When a load-in, set-up, strike, or load-out is not required the sections designated for those headings can be used for notes.

A sample of a special events listing follows:

#	DAY & DATE	TIME	DESCRIPTION	PLACE	LOAD IN SET UP	STRIKE LOAD OUT
9	Fri. 6/2/82	10:00 AM	K. Race/ TV interview	WXKD 14 W. 78th St.	*See note	
10	Fri. 6/2/82	2:00 PM	Puppet Show	Jefferson HS 421 Elm St.	12 Noon	3:00 PM

NOTES: *Miss Mary Johnson of WXKD will pick Kathy up at 9:15 and take her to the station.

It is important to know the amount of time open between bookings, the distance that has to be traveled, and the approximate amount of time required to make the trip. Without this information it is difficult to determine if it is possible to play both engagements, to know if the crews have to travel all night in order to get the production assembled in time for the next scheduled performance, etc.

The following example illustrates an instance in which the cast made an overnight stop, whereas the crew traveled the entire distance in one day to start the load-in and set-up the following morning:

DATES OF NEXT BOOKING 6/8/82 to 6/11/82   **LOCATION** Pittsburgh, PA

DISTANCE 350 miles   **APPROXIMATE TIME** 7½ hours

DATE & TIME OF FIRST COMMITMENT AT NEXT BOOKING 6/8/82, 8 PM

	CAST	CREW
DEPARTURE	3:00 PM, 6/7/82	11:00 AM, 6/7/82
TRANSPORTATION	Chartered bus	Truck & station wagon
OVERNIGHT STOP	Holiday Inn, Columbus, OH	Ramada Inn, Pittsburgh, PA
RESUME TRAVEL	10:00 AM, 6/8/81	None
MUST ARRIVE BY	4:00 PM, 6/8/82	9:00 AM, 6/8/82

This form aids in planning the tour before going on the road and while the tour is in progress. It should be updated or revised when playing the engagement and saved for use in planning future tours.

TOUR ITINERARIES (Forms 5-H & 5-I)

If the company has a company manager it is usually his responsibility to make arrangements for the company's transportation and hotel accommodations. The stage manager and company manager should work together to create an itinerary for the company. This is a chronological listing of the dates and locations of each engagement with whatever additional information will be needed by each member of the company.

Tour itineraries vary and may include any or all of the following information: days and dates of each engagement; travel notes; addresses and phone numbers of theatres the company will be playing and hotels where they will be staying; listings of shows, events, or commitments of the company and their times; and any notes pertaining to the engagement. Notes might include hotel prices, the distance of the hotel from the theater, etc.

Forms 5-H and 5-I are only suggested formats; before the start of any tour it should be decided what information will be included and what format will be used.

TOURING PERFORMANCE SCHEDULES (Form 5-J)

Form 5-J can be used to record the performance schedules of any touring company, and it is particularly useful for rotating repertory companies. The production record of each show should be a complete and separate entity. Form 5-J is self-explanatory, therefore no diagram will be included.

TOURING REHEARSAL SCHEDULES (Form 5-K)

Although a record of all rehearsals held on tour should be entered on the daily report sheet and a copy of the complete rehearsal schedule entered in the production book, it is often helpful to keep separate listings of this information so the stage manager can quickly establish the date, location, total length, and purpose of the rehearsal. Such a record is usually consulted as a guide for scheduling rehearsals on future tours, used as a reference should a dispute arise regarding overtime payment, etc.; therefore, it is not necessary that it be extremely detailed.

The following is an example of Form 5-K:

DATE	TIME	CITY & STATE	PLACE	REHEARSAL & PURPOSE
7/10/82	2 - 5 PM	Baton Rouge, LA	Haskell Hall	Act III (Hamlet) -- Brush up
7/12/82	2:30 - 5 PM	" " "	" " "	Puck scenes (Dream) -- Replacement of Puck

DAILY ATTENDANCE RECORD (Form 5-L)

A daily attendance record is frequently required during the rehearsal period of a production. The director may make changes in the schedule during a rehearsal. This may involve changing calls for the entire company, excusing an actor from a scene in order to use him at a later call, etc. If it is an Equity company it is important that the stage manager record these changes and either guarantee that length of rehearsals, breaks, etc. are not violated, or inform the general manager of overtime incurred by each actor so the appropriate overtime payments can be made.

An abbreviated sample of form 5-L follows:

ACTOR'S NAME	IN	OUT	IN	OUT	IN	OUT	PHOTO OR COSTUMES	TOTAL	OVER-TIME
K. Blair	10:00	3:00	4:30	7:00			---	7½	---
A. Cox	10:00	11:00	11:30	2:30	4:00	9:00	1 hr./C	9	1 hr.

WEEKLY ATTENDANCE RECORD (Form 5-M)

The weekly attendance record can usually replace the daily records once a production has opened. Form 5-M provides for separate entries of rehearsal and performance hours for each actor. A stage manager must work out his own system of abbreviations for recording weekly attendance.

An abridged sample of Form 5-M, using the first line for rehearsal hours and the second line for performances, follows:

ACTOR'S NAME	MONDAY	TUESDAY	WEDNESDAY	THURSDAY	FRIDAY			TOTAL
K. Blair	---	2B	4US	4B	2B			8B/4US
	E	E	E/Sam	E	E			+1
A. Cox	---	2B	---	5B	---			7B
	E	E	OUT	E	E			-1

KEY: B—Brush-up Rehearsal; E—Evening Performance In Own Role; E(Character)—Performed Understudy Role as (Character); US—Understudy Rehearsal; + —Played that number of performances in Understudy Role; − —Missed that number of performances

EMPLOYMENT TIME SHEET (Form 5-N)

During a particularly busy period it may become necessary for the company, or the stage manager personally, to hire some temporary help. These individuals may be paid a straight weekly salary or an hourly wage. When paying on an hourly basis it is often advisable to have the employee fill out a time sheet. This helps the employee keep track of the hours he is working and serves as a tax receipt for the employer. Form 5-N can be used for this purpose and should be self-explanatory.

FORM 5−A

SCHEDULING CALENDAR

PRODUCTION _____

MONTH _____ YEAR _____

Date _____

Page _____ of _____

SUNDAY	MONDAY	TUESDAY	WEDNESDAY	THURSDAY	FRIDAY	SATURDAY

FORM 5–B

PRODUCTION TIMETABLE

Date ———

PRODUCTION ———

Page ——— of ———

DAY	DATE	COSTUMES	LIGHTS	PROPS	SCENERY	SOUND

NOTES:

FORM 5–C

REHEARSAL TIME ALLOTMENT

Date _____   Page ____ of ____

COMPANY _____

DAY & DATE				
TOTAL				

TOTAL				

TOTAL				

KEY:

FORM 5–D

REHEARSAL SCHEDULE
Date _____

PRODUCTION _____   PLACE _____

TIME	

FORM 5–E

FORM 5–F

PHOTO CALL

Page ____ of ____

PRODUCTION _____

DATE _____ TIME _____ PLACE _____

#	ACT & SCENE	DESCRIPTION	ACTORS INVOLVED

NOTES:

FORM 5–G

BOOKING SCHEDULE & FACT SHEET

Date_____   Page_____ of_____

CITY & STATE _____   DATES _____

SPONSORING GROUP _____

LOCAL CONTACTS:
  (Name, Address, Phone)

THEATRE: HOTEL:

        TYPE OF THEATRE _____   UNION HOUSE _____

PERFORMANCES:

#	DAY & DATE	PERF. TIME	SHOW	LOAD IN SET UP	STRIKE LOAD OUT	NOTES

NOTES:

FORM 5–G (Side Two)

BOOKING SCHEDULE & FACT SHEET (Cont'd)

Date_____   Page_____ of_____

CITY & STATE _____ DATES _____

SPECIAL EVENTS:

#	DAY & DATE	TIME	DESCRIPTION	PLACE	LOAD IN SET UP	STRIKE LOAD OUT

NOTES:

TRAVEL INFO:

DATES OF NEXT BOOKING _____ LOCATION _____

DISTANCE _____ APPROXIMATE TIME _____

DATE & TIME OF FIRST COMMITMENT AT NEXT BOOKING _____

	CAST	CREW
DEPARTURE		
TRANSPORTATION		
OVERNIGHT STOP		
RESUME TRAVEL		
MUST ARRIVE BY		

NOTES:

FORM 5–H

Date _____

TOUR ITINERARY

PRODUCTION _____

Page ___ of ___

DAY & DATE	TRAVEL INFO	THEATRE INFO	SHOW/ EVENT	TIME	HOTEL INFO	NOTES

KEY:

FORM 5-I

TOUR ITINERARY

Date _____   Page ____ of ____

PRODUCTION _____

DAY & DATE	TRAVEL INFORMATION	THEATRE	HOTEL

FORM 5-I

FORM 5–J

TOURING
PERFORMANCE SCHEDULES

PRODUCTION _____

#	DATE	TIME	CITY & STATE	THEATRE	NOTES

FORM 5–K

Date _____

TOURING
REHEARSAL SCHEDULES

PRODUCTION _____

DATE	TIME	CITY & STATE	PLACE	REHEARSAL & PURPOSE

FORM 5−L

DAILY ATTENDANCE RECORD

PRODUCTION _____

ACTOR'S NAME	IN	OUT	IN	OUT	IN	OUT	PHOTO OR COSTUMES	TOTAL	OVER-TIME

FORM 5-M

WEEKLY ATTENDANCE RECORD

Week of _____

PRODUCTION _____

Page _____ of _____

ACTOR'S NAME										TOTAL	NOTES

KEY: *B* - Brush-up Rehearsal, *C* - Costume Call, *E* - Evening Performance, *M* - Matinee Performance, *P* - Photo Call, *PV* - Preview Performance, *R* - Replacement Rehearsal, *T* - Travel. *US* - Understudy Rehearsal, * - See Notes on Back

FORM 5-N

EMPLOYMENT TIME SHEET

COMPANY_____

NAME_____ FOR WEEK OF (   ) _____

ADDRESS _____ DEPARTMENT _____

_____ POSITION_____

NOTE: Please report all time to the nearest 1/4 hour

DAY	AM		PM		DAILY TOTAL
	IN	OUT	IN	OUT	
			TOTAL HOURS		

_____ _____ _____
Employee's Signature   Supervisor's Signature   Date

EMPLOYMENT TIME SHEET

COMPANY_____

NAME_____ FOR WEEK OF (   ) _____

ADDRESS _____ DEPARTMENT _____

_____ POSITION_____

NOTE: Please report all time to the nearest 1/4 hour

DAY	AM		PM		DAILY TOTAL
	IN	OUT	IN	OUT	
			TOTAL HOURS		

_____ _____ _____
Employee's Signature   Supervisor's Signature   Date

CHAPTER 6

Non-Technical Production Forms

CONTACT SHEET (Form 6–A)

"Contact Sheet" is a widely accepted term referring to information needed to contact a member of the company and any other persons or services connected with the production of theatre.

At an absolute minimum this list must contain the name, address, and telephone number of each entry. Other necessary information might be the role the person is playing, the position he holds with the company, or the contact information for his agent.

The stage manager's contact sheets should include *everyone* remotely connected with the production, rehearsal facilities, and theater, as well as outside persons and companies who have some connection with the production. This should include such things as supervising personnel of other groups using the company's facilities.

There are many different ways of organizing these sheets. The three most common are: (1) listing everyone alphabetically by name or service they provide; (2) using three separate sheets headed "Company," "Cast," and "Outside Services"; and (3) dividing headings into further categories—i.e., administrative personnel, technical personnel, designers, etc.

EXPENDITURES, RENTING & BORROWING
PETTY CASH EXPENDITURES (Form 6–B)

Handling of petty cash is usually a matter of company policy, and the stage manager's role in this regard can vary drastically from one company to another. In a resident company he may have to deal only with the expenditures of the stage managerial department, but in a road company he may have to control the flow of cash to all the technical departments as well.

One of the first items on the stage manager's check list when he joins a company should be to find out what the petty cash policy is and whether the company already has standard forms for that purpose. If they do not have forms, Form 6–B or a similar format can be used.

RUNNING RECORD OF EXPENDITURES (Form 6–C)

The purpose of this form is to maintain a record of all expenditures and to show at a glance where expenditures stand—how much money has been spent, the purpose of the expenditure, and what the present cash-in-hand situation is. The stage manager may also want to include the department for which the item was purchased, the place where it was obtained, the name of the person who purchased it, and the purchase order number. The company business manager should be consulted to find out if the purchase order system is used; if so, the stage manager should familiarize himself with the operating procedures.

How this form is used is a matter of company policy, budgeting systems, or preference of the stage manager. In a company with separate budgets for each department, it may be desirable to use a separate sheet for each; if this is the case, the "department" column can simply be omitted.

The beginning part of Form 6–C is self-explanatory and has therefore been omitted in the example below:

PURCHASED BY	AMOUNT PAID	CREDITS	BALANCE	P.O. #
---	---	$200.00	$200.00	---
H. Sticks	$ 6.00	---	$194.00	501
H. Sticks	$10.00	---	$184.00	502
H. Sticks	$ 3.00	---	$181.00	503

TRANSFER OF PETTY CASH (Form 6–D)

If the stage manager is providing cash to his assistants by transferring it from his account, he may prefer to keep his records on a transfer sheet while the assistants use a Running Record of Expenditures (Form 6–C) or Petty Cash (Form 6–B). If he also makes expenditures, he can transfer money to his own expense sheet.

In the following example of Form 6–D, L. Smith is the stage manager; H. Barney and B. Cross are assistants:

TRANSFERRED FROM	TRANSFERRED TO	AMOUNT	CREDITS	BALANCE
---	---	---	$100.00	$100.00
L. Smith	H. Barney	$25.00	---	$ 75.00
L. Smith	B. Cross	$72.00	---	$ 3.00
B. Cross	L. Smith	---	$ 8.41	$ 11.41
L. Smith	Expense Sheet	$10.00	---	$ 1.41

LONG DISTANCE PHONE LOG (Form 6–E)

Most theatre companies have such long and complicated phone bills that it is necessary for each department to keep a record of their long distance calls so that the general manager or business manager can easily check the bill.

Form 6–E was designed for this purpose and should be self-explanatory.

RECORD OF BORROWED ITEMS (Form 6–F)

The role the stage manager plays in borrowing items for company use may differ from one company to the next and may depend on the other functions he is performing in addition to being stage manager. In any event, it is always a good policy to keep track of everything that has been borrowed for use in a production or rehearsal and to request that all departments submit a list of such items to the stage manager.

After the production has closed this record will ensure that everything has been returned to its owner.

The stage manager should include on this form the number assigned to the borrowed item; a description of the item; the name, address, and phone number of the person who supplied the item; the date it was received by the company and the date on which the company has agreed to return it. "Notes" on the form may be used to record special requests from the owner, the condition of the item when received, acknowledgments made to the owner, as well as any damage done to the item and what is being done about it, the actual date the item was returned, etc.

RECORD OF RENTED ITEMS *(Form 6-G)*

Information in the record of borrowed items can also be included in the record of rented items. The major difference between borrowing and renting is the matter of payment. Headings of "Terms" and "Amount" should be added for rented items.

The stage manager must be sure that he understands exactly what the terms are and that the return date has been calculated properly. Keeping two hundred lighting instruments one day beyond the return date could result in the producer having to pay an entire week's or month's additional rental.

PLOT PROGRESSIONS (Forms 6-H & 6-I)

It is often useful to keep a brief record of the plot progression in a play. With some plays it may require only a few days to recall exactly where a certain event occurs; others may be so complicated by subplots, disguises, etc. that it may be desirable to consult a plot reference.

Form 6-H can be used as a quick reference for any play, as in the following example:

ACT/SCENE	PAGES	LOCATION	YEAR/ MONTH	TIME OF DAY	PLOT
I,1	1-8	A street in Verona	Mid-July 1650	9:10 AM	1. Street brawl between the houses of Montague and Capulet 2. Prince decrees that any further fighting will mean death 3. Benvolio tries to take Romeo's mind off of Rosaline

Form 6-I works well for complicated plots. The following example shows a plot progression with a separation of plot and subplot:

ACT/SCENE & PAGES	KATHARINA--PETRUCHIO PLOT	BIANCA--LUCENTIO SUB-PLOT
II,1 34-50	1. Kate abuses Bianca 2. Petruchio makes known to Baptista his wish to marry Kate	1. Bianca is abused by Kate 3. Lucentio (Cambio) and Hortensio (Licio) are accepted as tutors 4. Tranio (Lucentio) makes it known that he comes to woo Bianca

PRODUCTION & PUBLICITY PHOTOS (Form 6-J)

Production and publicity photos are a very important part of any production's visual record. They can be particularly useful in long-run productions to check that changes have not crept in gradually or to determine the amount of wear and tear on an item. They are also useful in touring companies to double check set-ups or replace publicity photos that never arrived.

The photographer or public relations director may have numbered the photos before the stage manager receives them. If not, it is advisable to do so. Each photo should also be dated on the back and attached to any corresponding captions or press releases.

Form 6–J can be used as an inventory and description sheet for production pictures as illustrated in the following example:

#	DESCRIPTION	ACTORS (Left to Right)
1	Set for Act I, Scene 1	None
2	I,1 Sword fight TYBALT: "What, drawn and talk of peace? I hate the word, as I hate hell, all Montagues, and thee. Have at thee, coward!"	George Willis (Tybalt) Fred Jones (Benvolio)

PROGRAM INFORMATION
PROGRAM COPY (Form 6–K)

Frequently it is the stage manager's responsibility to collect basic program information and give it to the person who oversees the program. Finding out who this person is and what information will be needed is another item that should be included on the stage manager's check list when joining a company.

Since it is important that everyone's name appear in the program as he wants it, the stage manager must be sure that any information he submits is accurate. Form 6–K can be used for this purpose. The form should not be thrown away once the information has been passed on, however, as the stage manager may be asked to proofread the program before final printing, and letting a mistake pass in proofing is as bad as submitting the information incorrectly.

In the following abbreviated example the first name was correct but the second required correction:

NAME	ROLE/POSITION	OK	CORRECTION	OK
Mary Ann Arras	Aunt Lilly	*maa*		
~~Connie Jones~~	Lotte		Constance Jones	*cj*

PROGRAM APPROVAL SHEET (Form 6–L)

The company may have its own program approval sheet, and if so, that should be used. No two productions will ever have exactly the same personnel and this should be kept in mind when putting together an approval sheet.

With the exception of the cast list, the stage manager is not usually responsible for the order of listing personnel and need not waste time fussing with it.

The following comments and suggestions are in reference to Form 6–L. (Please note the form consists of four pages.) The boxes on the left can be used as a check off point when the information has been acquired and checked for accuracy. The long blank lines are for additional entries.

If a position on the form is not applicable to the current production, it is a good idea to enter "None" on the corresponding line. This will indicate that it has not been accidentally overlooked.

The lines at the bottom of the first page can be used for the signatures needed to approve the completed information.

The "Performance Info" indicated on the fourth page may vary greatly from one production to another. For instance, there would not be enough space to list each scene of a Shakespearean play individually. In this type of situation the entry "See Attached" can be written in that area and a separate sheet containing the information included.

The final section deals with additional information that may be attached to the approval sheet before it is submitted to the publicity department.

PROGRAM ACKNOWLEDGMENTS (Form 6-M)

Program acknowledgments are also frequently referred to as "credits" or as "credits and acknowledgments." They are lists of individuals, companies, organizations, etc., who have provided items or performed services at a discount rate or free of charge; or suppliers who have contracted that they be acknowledged for items or services purchased by the company.

It is sometimes the stage manager's responsibility to see that this information is collected from the various departments and submitted with the program copy. By taking a quick glance over the forms for borrowed items (6-F) and rented items (6-G), the stage manager can check that the listings are complete.

Form 6-M does not require special discussion. Notes on this form may include, for example, what has been done to thank the person or company for their generosity.

REVIEWS & PUBLICITY (Forms 6-N & 6-O)

It is often desirable to make the production book a *complete* record of the production. In this case, at least the reviews and publicity pertaining to the production should be included. It is nice to have the articles, reviews, flyers, posters, etc., in the production book, but on an extensive tour with many bookings or a long-run production, this may amount to several volumes of material.

Form 6-N can be used to list this information when the production is stationary. Form 6-O was designed for touring productions.

ROOM ASSIGNMENTS (Forms 6-P & 6-Q)

Form 6-P is useful for productions that are playing one theatre for an extended engagement. It may also be used to indicate the locations of various departments—i.e., wardrobe, hair dressers, stage managers, etc.

Form 6-Q is a grid that can be used for various types of temporary room assignments, such as hotel rooms or dressing rooms on tour.

Below is a brief example of one way this form can be used:

	Holiday Pitts, PA	Ramada Colmbs, OH	Front Chicago, IL
F. Bruce	802	534	209
K. Calley	803	541	308

RUNNING ORDER & ACTOR'S PERSONAL SHEETS

The running order is a sequential listing by act and scene of the events which transpire during each scene. The purpose of this list is to let the actors know at a glance, as soon as possible after making an exit, what happens next.

At minimum this should contain the number of the act and scene, the location of the scene, all musical and dance numbers (if it is a musical), or some indication of what happens during that scene (if it is a non-musical). Sometimes a list of actors in each scene should be included.

Large, neat, legible charts containing this information should be posted in both wings, passageways from the dressing rooms, or wherever they are most accessible for the cast.

It might be helpful to print the running order on standard size paper since an actor may want to post a copy in his dressing room or take it home to study.

A partial sample of a typical format for a running list appears below:

I, 1   <u>Ladies' Dressing Room</u>

        1. Here we go again! — Louise, Maggie, and Female Chorus

        2. Why — Louise

I, 2   <u>Paul's Apartment</u>

        1. Why (1st Reprise) — Paul

An actor's personal sheets are expanded versions of the running list. They may also include the opening line of the scene, a warning cue for the end of the scene, the last line of the scene, the length of the scene, etc. Their main purpose is to give the actors a hard copy of the running order with space to make their own notations on items such as cue lines, entrances, costume changes, etc.

Skipping the entries for "Pre-Show" and "Overture," the following is an example of a possible format for personal sheets:

I, 1   (Ladies' Dressing Room)

       MAGGIE: "So I said to him, 'Listen, Georgie...' "

       Here We Go Again!

       Why

Warn: REBECCA: "Don't look at me!"
End :   SAM: "Ladies, you're on."   5 min., 6 sec.

Scene Change (Music Cover — "Here We Go Again!")

SCENE BREAKDOWNS

A scene breakdown is a listing of the characters appearing in each scene. Some directors prefer to make up the scene breakdown themselves and others prefer to have the stage manager do it for them. A scene breakdown should never be shown to anyone until it has the director's approval.

The director may indicate a particular format he wants used. If he doesn't, the stage manager may choose whatever format he prefers.

The information on a scene breakdown may vary, but it must at least include the character names and act and scene numbers. It is often helpful to include the page numbers, the location of each scene, a "pet name" for the scene, or something which will immediately identify it.

GRIDS (Forms 6–R & 6–S)

Using a grid is an effective way of making a scene breakdown. By listing the characters vertically and the scenes horizontally (or vice versa), the stage manager can simply check the box which corresponds to the correct character and scene.

The following is an abbreviated example of Form 6-R:

	Sonya	Fred	Peter	Natalie	Sally	Richard									
I,1 (1-15) Exposition	✓	✓	✓												
I,2 (15-30) Party		✓		✓	✓	✓									

Form 6–S is a horizontal layout of the same format.

CHARACTER GROUPINGS (Form 6-T)

Some directors prefer to have scene breakdowns indicating various character groupings. This is probably most common when there are two, three, or more separate factions.

An example of this type of scene breakdown is illustrated below:

ACT & SCENE	PAGES	NOBILITY	ARTISANS	FAIRY KINGDOM
V, 1 Play	81-86	Theseus Hippolyta Philostrate Hermia Lysander Demetrius Helena	Quince Snug Bottom Flute Snout Starveling	Fairy Puck Oberon Oberon's Train Titania Titania's Train

SCRIPT ASSIGNMENTS

AUDITION SCRIPTS

Please refer to Chapter 2 and Form 2-I for information on temporary assignment of scripts.

PERMANENT SCRIPT ASSIGNMENTS (Form 6-U)

It is important to keep a record of which scripts have been assigned to whom. It may be necessary to identify a script that was left behind in rehearsal, "call back" a script, etc.

Some companies will allow their members to keep their scripts once a production has closed; others prefer to have them returned. If the scripts have been rented it is mandatory that they be returned or paid for. Before releasing any scripts the stage manager should find out what the policy is regarding their return.

It is best to have the person accepting the script sign it out personally (this eliminates any question as to whether or not he ever received the script) and sign it in personally (this relieves him of any responsibility should it be lost after he's returned it).

Form 6–U was designed for the purpose of assigning scripts and should be self-explanatory. It can also be used for sides, vocal parts, scores, etc., by simply changing the heading of the sheet.

SCRIPT CHANGES (Form 6–V)

When large changes are made it is advisable to re-type these pages, especially in new plays or when scenes have been drastically edited or rewritten.

When a small change is made in a published text it is usually a waste of time, energy, and paper to rewrite the entire page. These changes should be recorded, however, and distributed to everyone involved in the production.

Form 6–V can be used to record changes in several ways. If recorded by act and scene, the entry can be made at the top of the sheet and the date information entered in the first column. If recorded by date, that information should appear at the top of the page and act and scene information in the first column.

It is often handy to work out a system of abbreviations to indicate the type of change being made (i.e., A—Addition, C—Cut, CH—Change). Any abbreviations used should be noted on the "Key".

Methods for recording script changes are illustrated in the following abbreviated examples:

JOHN: Mary, I thought I told you not to wear that dress any more.
MARY: I know, darling, but . . .

CHANGE	PAGE #	CHARACTER	SPEECH #	DESCRIPTION
Change	8	John	1st	CHANGE "I thought I told you"
				TO "I distinctly told you"
Cut	8	John	1st	"any more"
Add	8	John	1st	AFTER "wear that dress"
				ADD "Well, didn't I?"

The speech would now read as follows:

JOHN: Mary, I distinctly told you not to wear that dress. Well, didn't I?
MARY: I know, darling, but . . .

MISCELLANEOUS FORMS

BLANK FORMS (Forms 6-W & 6-X)

It is impossible to anticipate all the possible elements in a production and design appropriate forms and formats for each. Forms 6-W and 6-X have been included to provide a head start when designing new forms or making large modifications of the ones in this book.

The stage manager should not hesitate to design new forms when needed. A form is a tool, a means to an end, and should only be used when applicable and convenient.

SIGNS & CARDS (Forms 6-Y & 6-Z)

The "Rehearsal In Progress" sign has been designed to fit into the production book and can be kept there until needed.

The director may request that the stage manager let him know in advance when he is coming to the end of a rehearsal period so he can begin bringing things to a close. A relatively unobtrusive way to do this is to lay a card indicating the proper time in front of the director. It may be convenient to put these on three-by-five-inch cards and store them in a plastic notebook pocket or pouch in the production book or prompt script.

FORM 6-A

CONTACT SHEET

PRODUCTION _____

NAME	ROLE/POSITION	ADDRESS	PHONE	AGENT

FORM 6-B

PETTY CASH EXPENDITURES

Department ————————

PRODUCTION ————————

PLEASE NOTE: All entries must be accompanied by a receipt of purchase.

DATE	ITEM OR SERVICE PURCHASED	PURCHASED FROM	PURCHASED BY	AMOUNT
			TOTAL	

Submitted By ———————— Date ————————

Reimbursed By ———————— Date ———————— Amount ————————

FORM 6–C

PRODUCTION _____

Page ___ of ___

DATE	DEPT	ITEM/SERVICE PURCHASED	PURCHASED FROM	PURCHASED BY	AMOUNT PAID	CREDITS	BALANCE	P.O. #

FORM 6–D

TRANSFER OF PETTY CASH

TRANSFERRED FROM	PRODUCTION _____ TRANSFERRED TO	AMOUNT	CREDITS	BALANCE

FORM 6–D

FORM 6-E

LONG DISTANCE PHONE LOG

PRODUCTION ———

NAME	DATE	TIME	TELEPHONE #	PARTY CALLED	REASON FOR CALL	LENGTH

FORM 6–F

Department _____

RECORD OF BORROWED ITEMS

Page ___ of ___

PRODUCTION _____

#	DESCRIPTION	FROM	DATE RECEIVED	RETURN DATE	NOTES

FORM 6–G

PRODUCTION ⸻

RECORD OF RENTED ITEMS

#	DESCRIPTION	RENTED FROM	DATE RECEIVED	TERMS	AMOUNT	RETURN DATE

FORM 6–H

Date _____

PRODUCTION _____

ACT/SCENE	PAGES	LOCATION	YEAR/MONTH	TIME OF DAY	PLOT

FORM 6–1

PLOT PROGRESSION

PRODUCTION _____

ACT/SCENE & PAGES	

FORM 6–J

PRODUCTION & PUBLICITY PHOTOS

Date _____   Page ____ of ____

PRODUCTION _____

#	DESCRIPTION	ACTORS (Left to Right)

FORM 6-K

PROGRAM COPY

PRODUCTION _____

Page ____ of ____
Date ____

NAME	ROLE/POSITION	OK	CORRECTION	OK	DATE

FORM 6-L

Date _____ Page _____ of _____

PROGRAM APPROVAL SHEET

PRODUCTION _____

Based On _____

Adapted From _____

☐ Playwrights _____

☐ Translators _____

☐ Composers _____

☐ Lyricists _____

☐ Producers _____

_____

☐ Artistic Director _____

☐ General Manager _____

☐ Assistant _____

☐ Company Manager _____

☐ Assistant _____

☐ Theatre _____

_____

☐ Director _____

☐ Assistant _____

☐ Choreographer _____

☐ Assistant _____

☐ Musical Director _____

☐ Assistant _____

☐ Dance Music Arranged By _____

☐ Orchestrated By _____

☐ Incidental Music By _____

☐ Sword Play Staged By _____

☐ Scenic Designer _____

☐ Assistant _____

☐ Lighting Designer _____

☐ Assistant _____

☐ Costume Designer _____

☐ Assistant _____

☐ _____

☐ _____

☐ _____

_____ _____

(Production Stage Manager) (Director)

FORM 6–L (Side Two)

PROGRAM APPROVAL SHEET

Date_____   Page_____ of _____

PRODUCTION_____

- ☐ Makeup_____
- ☐ Hair _____
- ☐ Sound _____
- ☐ Properties _____
- ☐ Special Effects _____
- ☐ Production Manager _____
- ☐ Production Stage Manager _____
- ☐ Stage Manager _____
- ☐ Assistant Stage Managers _____
- ☐ Dance Captain _____
- ☐ Fencing Master_____
- ☐ Production Assistants _____

  _____

- ☐ Production Secretaries_____
- ☐ Casting Director _____
- ☐ Press Representatives _____

  _____

- ☐ Advertising Representatives _____

  _____

- ☐ Public Relations Director _____
- ☐ Legal Counsel _____
- ☐ House Manager _____
- ☐   Assistant _____
- ☐ Accountants _____
- ☐ House Physician _____
- ☐ Merchandising _____
- ☐ Insurance _____
- ☐ Group Sales _____

  _____

  _____

- ☐ _____
- ☐ _____
- ☐ _____
- ☐ _____
- ☐ _____
- ☐ _____
- ☐ _____

PROGRAM APPROVAL SHEET (Cont'd)

Date_____   Page_____ of _____

PRODUCTION_____

SCENERY:
□ Master Carpenter _____
_____
_____
_____
_____
_____

PROPERTIES:
□ Master Propertyman_____
_____
_____
_____
_____

COSTUMES:
□ Wardrobe   Supervisor_____
_____
_____
_____
_____

LIGHTS:
□ Master Electrician_____
_____
_____
_____
_____

SOUND:
□ Chief Technician_____
_____
_____
_____
_____

Scenery Constructed By_____
Costumes Constructed By _____
Wigs By _____
Light Equipment By _____
Sound Equipment By_____

PROGRAM APPROVAL SHEET (Cont'd)

Date_____   Page_____ of _____

PRODUCTION_____

MUSICIANS:

☐ _____

_____

_____

_____

_____

_____

_____

_____

_____

_____

_____

PERFORMANCE INFO:

ACT & SCENE	TIME	PLACE

Number of Intermissions_____   Length of Intermissions_____

Original Production: Date _____

Place _____

ADDITIONAL INFO:

ATTACHED: Cast List_____   Credits & Acknowledgments_____   Bios_____

Director's Notes_____   Musical Numbers_____   Understudy List_____

FORM 6–M

PROGRAM ACKNOWLEDGMENTS

Department ___

PRODUCTION ___

NAME TO BE ACKNOWLEDGED	ADDRESS & PHONE	FOR	NOTES

FORM 6–N

Date _____   Page ____ of ____

PRODUCTION _____

DATE OF ARTICLE	NEWSPAPER OR PUBLICATION	DESCRIPTION & NOTES

FORM 6–O

Date _____

REVIEWS & PUBLICITY

PRODUCTION _____

Page _____ of _____

DATE OF PERF.	CITY & STATE	THEATRE	DATE OF ARTICLE	NEWSPAPER OR PUBLICATION	ADDITIONAL PUBLICITY

FORM 6–P

Date _____   Page ____ of ____

DRESSING ROOM ASSIGNMENTS

PRODUCTION _____

NUMBER	ACTOR'S NAME	ROLE PLAYING

FORM 6–Q

ROOM ASSIGNMENTS

COMPANY _____

FORM 6–R

SCENE BREAKDOWN

Date _____ Page ____ of ____

PRODUCTION _____

FORM 6–R

FORM 6-S

PRODUCTION _____

SCENE BREAKDOWN

FORM 6-T

SCENE BREAKDOWN

PRODUCTION _____

ACT & SCENE	PAGES	

FORM 6-U

SCRIPT ASSIGNMENTS

PRODUCTION _____

Page ____ of ____

#	SIGNED OUT BY	DATE	SIGNED IN BY	DATE	PHONE #	ROLE/POSITION

DATE _____

<u>SCRIPT CHANGES</u>

PRODUCTION _____

Page ____ of ____

DATE/ ACT, SCN	CHANGE	PAGE #	CHARACTER	SPEECH #	DESCRIPTION

KEY: A—Addition, C—Cut, CH—Change

FORM 6–W

Date_____

Page____of____

PRODUCTION_____

FORM 6–X

PRODUCTION _____

QUIET PLEASE

REHEARSAL IN

PROGRESS

5 MIN.

10 MIN.

TIME

BREAK

CHAPTER 7

Starting Technical Notes

The remaining portion of this book deals with technical forms and formats. It is essential that the stage manager maintain up-to-date copies of all plots, cue sheets, and technical notes. In prerehearsal and rehearsal periods the early notes and plots will serve as a guide and check list in the development of the technical elements. Once the production has reached the stage of final techs and performances, copies should be kept to check that everything is happening as originally planned.

The stage manager should have duplicate copies of *every* plot, cue sheet, running list, or technical list that affects the production. This ensures that, should a set of notes be lost by one of the departments, the show can continue with one of the stage manager's copies. If for instance, the electrician takes the cue sheets home to recopy them and has a serious accident on the way to the theatre, the manager should be able to give another electrician a copy of his lighting cue sheets. Not having duplicate copies of all plots, cue sheets, etc., is the equivalent of not having copies of the script for the understudies or standbys. Duplicate information can also aid the assistant stage manager or replacement stage manager if he has to take over the production, and a copy of the material from the original production can be extremely useful in starting another company of the same production.

When the technical information deals with notes pertaining to actors, it is wise to use character names rather than actors' names. There are two primary reasons for this: the technical staff has not been with the production as long as other members of the company and will naturally learn character names first, and the actor playing the role may change. If the stage manager made entries on technical plots using the actor's name, he would have to change every entry pertaining to that person should the actor leave the company. The use of character names also helps avoid confusion when starting a second company.

NOTES FROM THE SCRIPT

Notes from the script are exactly those notes pertaining to technical elements extracted from the script. By getting this work done early, the stage manager will have more time for other important tasks once rehearsals begin.

It is important that the stage manager double check to make sure he has the correct edition or translation of the script before plunging into this type of work. The director should then be consulted to find out if he intends to make any major modifications—i.e., a change of period, location, etc. With this information the stage manager can start thinking along the same lines as the director and make the appropriate adjustments.

A simple way to utilize these forms is to put them into a three-ring binder with tabbed dividers for each heading—scenery, props, costumes, lights, and sound. If the director wants the stage manager to assume responsibility for making the scene breakdown, this is a convenient time to do so. (See Forms 6R–T—Scene Breakdown.)

These notes should record all information supplied by the playwright and any other items that appear necessary to the production. The stage direction ''Romeo draws his sword'' mentions only a sword, but it is a fair assumption that he has a scabbard, belt, and/or halter. These items should be included and marked with some kind of symbol to indicate that a logical deduction has been made. A possible symbol might be ''(?).'' A major alteration, such as a change in period, will require more generalizing on the part of the stage manager. For example, a production of ''Romeo and Juliet'' updated to 1960 probably would not call for the use of swords. Unless it is known from the start what type of adjustments are being made, the stage manager may have to generalize with ''Weapon.'' This leaves it open for the director to decide if he wants to use knives, pistols, machine guns, or whatever.

It is advisable to use separate sheets for each act, and if the show is extremely heavy technically, for each scene. Each sheet should be clearly marked to indicate the act or scene from which the notes were taken.

When several departments are concerned with the same item (i.e., a piece of furniture which the scenic designer will select or design, but the property master will purchase or build), the notes pertaining to that item should be entered for all departments concerned. It is suggested that when this type of double notation occurs the stage manager indicate it in some way. A set of abbreviations may be used for this purpose such as, ''Also Listed in the Following Notes: *c—Costumes, *l—Lights, *p—Props, *sc—Scenic, *s—Sound.''

The excerpt below demonstrates how notes can be extracted from the script and organized on Forms 7-A to 7-E:

ACT III   Page 54

The living room of the Johnsons' home in London. An evening in October 1902. BEN sits on the settee DR smoking his pipe and reading the London Times, while ANGELA — in a pink lace dressing gown — stares dreamily at the fire blazing in the tile fireplace. Just as the mantle clock strikes 7:00, TOM ANDERSON bursts through the french doors UC.

The above passage gives enough information to make the following notations:

PLACE: The Johnsons' living room   TIME: 7:00 PM
         London, England   October 1902

SCENIC ELEMENTS (Form 7-A)

PAGE	SCENIC ELEMENT	PLACEMENT	DESCRIPTION & NOTES
54	Settee	DR	*p
54	Fireplace		Tile with fire and mantle to hold clock/ *p & *l
54	French Doors	UC	Must be practical

PROPS (Form 7–B)

PAGE	PROP	USED BY	PLACEMENT	DESCRIPTION & NOTES
54	Settee	Furniture	DR	*sc
54	Pipe	Ben		
54	Pipe tobacco (?)	Ben		
54	Matches (?)	Ben		
54	London Times	Ben		October 1902
54	Fireplace	Set piece		Tile w/ fire and mantle to hold clock/ *sc & *1
54	Clock		Mantle	If practical, must strike 7:00/ *s

COSTUMES (Form 7–C)

PAGE	CHARACTER	COSTUME	DESCRIPTION & NOTES
54	Angela	Dressing gown	Pink lace

LIGHTING (Form 7–D)

PAGE	TYPE OF NOTE	DESCRIPTION & NOTES
54	Time of day	7:00 PM
54	Time of Year	October
54	Effect	Fire burning in fireplace/ *sc & *p

SOUND (Form 7–E)

PAGE	EFFECT	DESCRIPTION & NOTES
54	Clock Striking	Mantle clock striking 7:00/ *p

Obviously the above notes are not complete, but they do take into consideration everything that the playwright mentioned (i.e., settee, pipe, dressing gown, etc.) and several items that will be needed for an actor to complete the business that the playwright has assigned him (i.e., pipe tobacco and matches).

As illustrated in the previous examples, the mention of the fire and fireplace require a triple notation. The scenic designer will either have to locate a fireplace or design one, the property master will have to build or buy one, and the lighting designer will have to work out the fire effect if it is done electrically. If the fire is real, the entire responsibility falls to the property department. The stage manager does not have the authority to decide whether or not the playwright's directions will be followed—the director will make that decision. Nor does he have the authority to stipulate the manner in which the effect will be achieved. Such items must be discussed in production meetings between the director, designers, and heads of each department. By noting the fire on both prop and lighting notes, the stage manager has ensured that both departments realize the responsibility for this item either has to be shared or assigned to one.

WORKING NOTES (Forms 7–F to 7–K)

After double checking the notes from the script, the working notes can be started. These are basically the same format as the notes from the script with space for recording additional notes during rehearsals or production meetings. Since script notes are usually recorded in the order they are mentioned, it may be desirable to rearrange entries for the working notes. (Act I's prop list, for instance, may start with furniture, then dishware, soft goods, etc.); or it may be desirable to record all the costumes for one character on the same sheet, indicating when each is worn. Form 7–H has been designed specifically for the purpose of recording notes by character.

It may be a good idea to type these notes since typing requires less space and later can be copied and distributed to the various technical departments. Once the stage manager has collected as much information as possible from the script, he can begin working with the director to expand or modify his notes. If time permits, these notes can be updated and copies made for the director, designers, and heads of each department prior to design conferences and production meetings where they can serve as a basic outline for the discussions.

The forms for the working notes are very similar to the forms used to record notes from the script and, therefore, require no illustration of their use. Since these are working forms it is usually a good idea to leave extra space in each act and scene for additional entries.

FORM 7–A

SCENIC NOTES—FROM SCRIPT

Act _____ Scene _____

PLACE:

PRODUCTION
TIME: _____ NOTES: _____

Date _____

Page _____ of _____

PAGE	SCENIC ELEMENT	PLACEMENT	DESCRIPTION & NOTES

KEY:

FORM 7–B

PROP NOTES—FROM SCRIPT

Act _____ Scene _____   Page _____ of _____

PLACE: PRODUCTION   Date _____
                          TIME: _____

                                          NOTES:

PAGE	PROP	USED BY	PLACEMENT	DESCRIPTION & NOTES

KEY:

FORM 7–C

COSTUME NOTES—FROM SCRIPT

Act _____ Scene _____

PLACE:

PRODUCTION
TIME: _____   NOTES:

Page _____ of _____

Date _____

PAGE	CHARACTER	COSTUME	DESCRIPTION & NOTES

KEY:

FORM 7–D

LIGHTING NOTES—FROM SCRIPT

Act ____ Scene ____

PLACE:

PRODUCTION
TIME: ____ NOTES: ____

Page ____ of ____

Date ____

PAGE	TYPE OF NOTE	DESCRIPTION & NOTES

KEY:

FORM 7–E

SOUND NOTES—FROM SCRIPT

Act _____ Scene _____

PLACE:

PRODUCTION
TIME:

NOTES:

Date _____

Page _____ of _____

PAGE	EFFECT	DESCRIPTION & NOTES

KEY:

FORM 7–F

WORKING SCENIC NOTES

Act _____ Scene _____

PLACE:

PRODUCTION
TIME: _____   NOTES:

Date _____

Page _____ of _____

PAGE	SCENIC ELEMENT	PLACEMENT	DESCRIPTION & NOTES	NOTES

KEY:

FORM 7–G

Act _____ Scene _____

PRODUCTION _____

PLACE: _____   TIME: _____   NOTES: _____

PAGE	PROP	USED BY	PLACEMENT	DESCRIPTION & NOTES	NOTES

KEY:

FORM 7–H

WORKING COSTUME NOTES

Character _____

PLACE: _____

PRODUCTION
TIME: _____   NOTES: _____

Date _____

Page ____ of ____

PAGE	ACT & SCENE	COSTUME	DESCRIPTION & NOTES	NOTES

KEY:

FORM 7–I

WORKING COSTUME NOTES

Act _____ Scene _____

PLACE:

PRODUCTION
TIME: NOTES:

Date _____

Page _____ of _____

PAGE	CHARACTER	COSTUME	DESCRIPTION & NOTES	NOTES

KEY:

FORM 7–J

Date_____

Page_____of_____

Act_____ Scene_____

PLACE:

PRODUCTION
TIME:_____ NOTES:_____

PAGE	TYPE OF NOTE	DESCRIPTION & NOTES	NOTES

KEY:

FORM 7-K

Act _____ Scene _____

PLACE:

PRODUCTION
TIME: _____   NOTES: _____

Date _____

Page _____ of _____

PAGE	EFFECT	DESCRIPTION & NOTES	DIRECTION	LENGTH	NOTES

KEY:

CHAPTER 8

Scenic Elements & Props

SCENERY PRESETS (Form 8-A)

It is extremely important that each piece of scenery be assigned an exact position at the top of the show. There are times when scenery and/or furniture will have to be struck from backstage and new pieces brought in during intermission. When this occurs, the new preset should also be recorded.

The stage manager should check the position of all set pieces before each performance and during each intermission to make sure they are all in the theater or readily accessible. Stagehands or actors changing the scenery may not have time to track down a missing piece during a shift. If the piece is not where it should be, the change may be held up or the show may have to continue without it. Also, improperly preset pieces may be a safety hazard to the actors and crews.

Probably the quickest way to check the onstage preset is to use a 1/4-inch ground plan. Diagrams of backstage, shop, and storage room presets may also be drawn.

Form 8-A can be used to record additional and more detailed information pertaining to presets. The following is an abbreviated example of how this form can be used for standing scenic units:

WHEN	WHERE	#	DESCRIPTION	SET BY
1 hour before curtain	Off S.R.C.	3-F	Act II, SR door unit	F. James

The following, an example of Form 8-A, describes the preset of a flying piece:

WHEN	WHERE	#	DESCRIPTION	SET BY
1 hour before curtain	Yellow trim	2-M/ line 58	Church window	H. Christian

The stage manager may decide to use separate sheets for standing pieces and hanging pieces.

The "#" heading on this form refers to the number that was assigned to the piece when it was constructed and should appear on the back of the scenic piece. For hanging pieces this heading can be used to indicate the "line" to which the piece has been assigned. It is not uncommon for one unit, such as a three-fold flat, to be assigned more than one number. When this happens the entire series should be noted—i.e., "1-A, 1-B, 1-C" or "1 A-C". If these numbers have not been assigned, the stage manager or master carpenter should do so before going into technical rehearsals. This will eliminate any possible confusion of identical or similar pieces.

Notes on this sheet may include the act and scene in which the piece is used, details for presetting the piece (i.e., "Door must be bolted"), pre-show preparation for upcoming shifts (i.e., a line must be flown in, a curtain untied, and the line again flown out), etc.

This form should also indicate the storage position of pieces until the next performance.

MASTER SHIFT PLOT (Form 8-B)

The master shift plot should record the movement of all scenic elements during the performance. It is advisable to have this plot worked out as completely as possible before technical rehearsals begin to avoid confusion when rehearsing the shifts. It is a good idea to number, letter, or name each shift so that everyone involved can identify it immediately. Unless each shift is recorded separately, the sheet should be clearly marked to indicate what each shift consists of and where one ends and another begins.

Form 8-B is an example of a master shift plot. "From/To" can be used to indicate the act, scene, and location before and after the shift. For example, "FROM: I, 1—Garden/TO: I, 2—Living Room." "Places" means the crew should get into position for the upcoming shift; "cue" refers to the actual beginning of the shift.

The following is an example of several sample entries on Form 8-B:

PERFORMED BY	ENTER	SHIFT (Set, Strike, Move, Etc.)	TO	EXIT
J. Dicks	SL	Strike UC door unit (11-G) w/ H Cole	Off SR	In 3 SR
	In 1 SR	Set DR door unit (12-D) w/ H. Cole	DR spike marks (red)	In 1 SR
T. Elm	---	Fly IN line #30 -- Curtain	Green trim	---
	---	Fly OUT line #17 -- Window	White trim	---

Notes, which can be made under the "Shift" heading of this form, might consist of the timing of entrances and exits with another person, the name of another crew member shifting the same piece, etc.

SHIFT CHARTS

When working with non-union crews it is often helpful to make a shift chart. This performs basically the same function for the crew as does the running order for the cast. It is a quick reference for crew members to check before the upcoming shift. Rather than the straight listing used for the running order, the shift chart employs a grid format. A large piece of cardboard (approximately two-by-three feet) is the best material to use in making a shift chart since the entries should be large, neat, and legible.

The chart should not be expected to replace copies of the shift assignment sheets; it is supplemental to them. The following information should be included on a shift chart: act, scene, location, cue to go to places for the shift, cue to start the shift, entrance and exit information, and a description of the duties assigned each crew member.

The information on the example of Form 8-B might appear on the shift chart as follows:

SHIFT	#1 1,1 — Garden TO 1,2 — Living Room	#2
PLACES	P. 27, FRANK: "Mary, wait for me!"	
CUE	Change lights start up	
J. Dicks	Enter SL, Strike UC Door Unit/11—G (w/ H. Cole), Exit SR3 Enter SR1, Set DR Door Unit/12—D on DR red spike marks, Exit SR1	
T. Elm	Fly IN — Line #30 — Curtain to Green Fly OUT — Line #17 — Window to White	

Please note that this format is only useful when all crew members are using the same cues.

SHIFT ASSIGNMENTS (Form 8–C)

Once the master shift plot has been worked out, shift assignment sheets can be completed. The purpose of these sheets is to provide each crew member a hard copy of all information pertaining to his shifts. He can carry it with him to use as a reference and make whatever extra notations are helpful. Since it contains only his assignments, he need not worry about accidentally getting them confused with another crew member's.

The following example illustrates how ones persons's assignments for the first two shifts might be entered on Form 8–C:

#	PLACES & CUE	ENTER	SHIFT (Set, Strike, Move, Etc.)	TO	EXIT
1	PLACES: p. 27 (I,1) FRANK: "Mary, wait for me!" CUE: Change lights start up	SL	Strike UC door unit/11-G (w/ H. Cole)	Off SR	In 3 SR
		In 1 SR	Set DR door unit/12-D (w/ H. Cole)	DR red spikes	In 1 SR
2	PLACES: p. 54 (I,2) MARY: "Yes, I saw you with her." CUE: House breaks for intermission	In 1 SR	Strike DR door unit/12-D (w/H. Cole)	Off SR	In 1 SR
		In 3 SR	Set SR banister/13-H	UR grn spikes	In 2 SL
		In 2 SL	Set SL banister/13-J	UL grn spikes	In 2 SL

SHIFT ASSIGNMENTS (HANGING ELEMENTS) (Form 8–D)

Since the mechanics of shifting scenery on the deck and flying scenery are different, it follows that the duties assigned to the flyman would differ from those of the grip.

Form 8–D has been designed for the shifting of curtains, scrims, drops, flying scenic pieces, etc. An example of information entered on that form follows:

SHIFT #	ACT & SCENE	PAGE	CUE		DESCRIPTION	NOTES
1	End I,1	29	WARN:	(p. 27) FRANK: "Mary, wait for me!"	IN -- Line #30 (grn) (house curtain)	Fast curtain
			CUE:	Blackout	OUT -- Line #17 (wht) (window unit)	Slowly, avoid light pipe

WORKING PROP PLOT (Form 8–E)

There is a common misconception (probably acquired from the information in the back of published scripts) that a prop plot is a listing of properties needed for the production. This list is merely an inventory, a necessary piece of information for a prop plot. By the same token, a preset and/or running list does not constitute a plot.

The plot should contain at least the following information for each prop: the number assigned to it, a description of it, an indication of when it is used, the name of the character who uses it, the place it is preset, a description of where it "travels" during the performance, and any special notes about the prop or its use.

Naturally all of the above information will have to be gathered during the course of rehearsals. It is advisable, therefore, to start with the description of the prop and the character who uses it, and proceed from there.

The following is an example of Form 8–E as it might appear when completed:

#	WHEN USED	ITEM	USED BY	PLACEMENT & MOVEMENT	NOTES
27	Act I	Riding crop	Regina & Sam	SR prop table/Reg gives to Sam, Sam strikes to SL prop table	
28	Act I	8" round silver tray	Nancy	SL prop table/dining table, Nancy strikes to SL prop table	Holds coffee pot, sugar bowl, creamer, & spoon

RUNNING PROP LIST

The information needed to preset the properties for each production and the duties of the property men before, during, and after the performance constitute the running prop list. Each running list is unique to the production for which it is used, but there are certain elements common to all. Most running lists start with the pre-show duties. These consist of presetting the props and such things as sweeping the stage, filling pitchers and wine bottles, making sandwiches, wrapping presents, etc. Diagrams of onstage presets and backstage prop tables are very helpful to both the propertyman for setting the show and the stage manager for checking the presets. These need not be elaborate or even to scale, but they must be accurate.

It is usually a good idea to start the preset list with whatever needs to be set onstage and then proceed to items for the prop tables, storage areas, dressing rooms, etc. The job of setting and checking props is made a lot easier if the presetting of props is dealt with in some kind of set pattern. For instance, the onstage preset might be listed from stage right to stage left, the prop table might contain all of the props for one actor in a designated area, etc.

Once the preshow information has been entered on the running list, it is best to move through the show chronologically, recording the specific assignments of the property department. This part of the list will consist of such things as checking that the actors have personal props, handing or taking props from actors on fast exits and entrances, executing live sound cues, making property changes during intermissions and scene shifts, etc.

After the show, duties such as clearing the stage, storing hand props, and washing dishes should also be recorded on the running list. The final entry should be a listing of the perishable or expendable items that may have to be replaced and chores that have to be done before the next performance—i.e., cleaning and pressing tablecloths and napkins.

Once the running list has been worked out, it should be no trouble to add a grid and make a check list for the propertyman if he desires one.

FURNITURE PLOTS

The furniture plot, like the running prop list, is indigenous to the particular production. In many respects it can be regarded as a combination preset list, running list, and shift and storage plot of the furniture pieces used in the production. Like the prop running list, it is helpful to incorporate diagrams and start with the preshow preset, working from the onstage items to those in the wings, shops, or storage areas. Once the preset information has been recorded, the remaining entries should be made chronologically. These entries include furniture moved by the actors onstage during the course of the play, changes made during scene shifts and intermissions, and rearrangement of furniture preset in the wings.

During scene shifts, furniture may either be left where it is, set, struck, or moved to a new position. All of the above information should be included on the furniture plot as well as the position of a piece that has been moved, set, or struck, and the name of the person who handles the piece along with the number assigned to it.

Numbers used to identify pieces on the furniture plot should be the same as those assigned to them on the master prop plot. The last entry on the furniture plot should indicate where each piece is stored until the next performance.

FORM 8–A

SCENERY PRESET

Date _____

PRODUCTION _____

Page ___ of ___

WHEN	WHERE	#	DESCRIPTION	SET BY	NOTES

FORM 8–B

MASTER SHIFT PLOT

Shift # _____

FROM _____

PLACES _____

PRODUCTION _____ TO _____ CUE _____

Page _____ of _____

Date _____

PERFORMED BY	ENTER	SHIFT (Set, Strike, Move, Etc.)	TO	EXIT

KEY:

FORM 8–C

Shift # _____ To # _____

Performed By _____

PRODUCTION _____

Page _____ of _____

Date _____

#	PLACES & CUE	ENTER	SHIFT (Set, Strike, Move, Etc.)	TO	EXIT

KEY:

FORM 8–D

SHIFT ASSIGNMENTS
(HANGING ELEMENTS)

Performed By _____

PRODUCTION _____

SHIFT #	ACT & SCENE	PAGE	CUE	DESCRIPTION	NOTES

KEY:

FORM 8-E

Date _____

PRODUCTION _____

Page ____ of ____

#	WHEN USED	ITEM	USED BY	PLACEMENT & MOVEMENT	NOTES

CHAPTER 9

Costumes

COSTUME DESCRIPTION CHART (Form 9–A)

A complete and detailed description of each costume is useful for several reasons. It can be extremely helpful in rehearsals for answering such questions as, "What color is her dress?"; "Is she wearing high heels?"; "How does that fasten?"; or "Does he have pockets in that coat?" Having this information can save the stage manager the trouble of tracking down the designer to learn the answer, returning to the director with the information, discovering that the director wants it changed, returning to the designer who says, "That won't work," etc. This kind of shuttling back and forth wears out the stage manager and wastes his time.

A costume description list can also be helpful to the actor during dress parades to help him locate his costume pieces, check that the costume is complete, and that he is wearing it properly. When an understudy takes over at the last minute, it is reassuring to know he has a check list for his costume needs.

The following example illustrates how the chart portion of Form 9–A can be used:

ARTICLE	COLORS	FABRIC	SIZE	HOW FASTEN	POCKETS	NOTES		
						CLEAN	PACK	
Panty hose	Cinnamon	Nylon	Small	Elastic/waist	None	Handwash	Cloth bag	
1-piece dress	Blue/wht	Crushed velvet	Fitted	Zipper/back	None	Dry clean	Hangs	

Information about how a costume should be packed is only needed when a show is touring. This area can be used for general notes when the show does not tour.

It may be convenient to work out a set of abbreviations for frequently used notations. The following are some possible suggestions: DC—Dry Clean, F—Fitted for Actor (See Measurement Chart), HW—Hand Wash, L—Launder, *—Personal Article Belonging to the Actor. Whenever abbreviations are used, they should be recorded on the "Key."

It is important that the stage manager have a record of all items worn by the actor. Since such items as undergarments, jewelry, and costume props can be easily overlooked, it is helpful to make a notation at the bottom of the form listing all of the items that should be included.

When a costume change involves only a few items, such as taking off an apron and putting on a hat and coat, it would be a waste of time to list again every costume piece the actor is wearing. This information can easily be recorded as follows:

> **SAME AS PREVIOUS COSTUME WITH FOLLOWING CHANGES:**
> **ADDITION OF:** Blue tweed coat   **REMOVAL OF:** White apron
> Blue felt hat

In this instance only the information pertaining to the coat and hat would have to be described on the chart.

The back of Form 9–A is a continuation of the front of the chart with additional information about makeup and costume changes. Onstage changes may consist of, for example, taking off a hat and coat and putting them on a coat tree. It is important to note these changes because wardrobe may have to return the clothing to the dressing room during intermission, move it to the sofa, etc.

Noting the next costume change for each actor on the description sheet can save the stage manager quite a bit of time making the change plot, master costume plot, and running list.

MASTER PRESET PLOT (Form 9–B)

The purpose of this form is to record information pertaining to all preset costume pieces. For a show with many preset pieces, it may be best to use a separate sheet for each act and scene requiring presets. When there are relatively few presets, a form similar to Form 9–B can be used.

The following is an example of several entries made on Form 9–B:

WHEN	WHERE	SET BY	FOR/CHARACTER	PIECES	NOTES
1 hour before curtain	Coat tree	K. James	Mr. Simpson	Black overcoat White muffler Black top hat	Overcoat set over muffler--US hook Hat--center spike
	SL change booth	Y. Neils	Mr. Everett	Green smoking jacket Brown leather slippers	Jacket--back of chai Slippers--under tabl
1st Interm.	Coffee table	K. James	Mr. Simpson	White gloves	USR end of table

The "Notes" section of this form may be used for specific cues for setting pieces, descriptions of the manner in which the item should be preset, etc.

A list of the preset costume pieces should appear on the stage manager's preshow and intermission check lists. If he wants an assistant to assume responsibility for checking the presets, he should be able to give out the master preset lists with confidence that the information is complete enough to answer any questions the assistant might have.

MASTER CHANGE PLOT (Form 9–C)

The master change plot is a record of all costume changes that are made from the time the show goes up until the final curtain falls. This plot should contain all changes, whether they occur in the dressing rooms, backstage, or onstage.

It is often helpful to number the changes. Some stage managers number them consecutively; others prefer to number the changes by character, using the character abbreviations in the prompt script followed by a number. For example, "M-2" could be easily identified as the second costume change made by the character Mary.

The following example of Form 9–C illustrates the third costume change for Kate from a production of "The Taming of the Shrew":

#	WHEN	WHERE	DRESSER/ CHARACTER	OFF	ON	AMOUNT OF TIME
3	III,2 p. 61 Kate's exit	Dressing room	J. Cummings/KATE	Tiara & veil Wedding wig All jewelry Wedding dress Clean petticoat Satin slippers	Dirty petticoat Dirty white dress Muddy slippers Ratty wig	10 min.

MASTER COSTUME PLOTS (Forms 9-D & 9-E)

The costume plot is the master chart of all information pertaining to use of costumes during a performance. The costume plot should tell the stage manager and wardrobe supervisor exactly what costume each actor is wearing at any given moment, what he has just taken off, what he is about to put on, when and if costume changes are made, etc. The information from the costume description sheets, presets, and change plot should be combined to make the master costume plot. Since one piece of paper is not large enough to accommodate all the information of the costume description and change plot, it is necessary that they work in conjunction with the master costume plot to create a complete picture. Preset costume pieces should be incorporated into the plot when they are worn. The plot should move through the show chronologically, listing the *complete* costume for every character in each scene.

The following is an example of the use of Form 9–D incorporating Kate's change cited in the previous section:

ACT & SCENE	CHARACTER	COSTUME	CHANGE #	WHEN	WHERE
III,2	KATE	Personal panties White corset White tights Clean white petticoat White wedding dress White satin slippers Tiara & white veil Blue sapphire necklace Gold earrings & bracelet Wedding wig	3	End II,2 p. 61	Dressing room
IV,1	PETRUCHIO	Personal undershorts White T-shirt 1 red stocking 1 yellow stocking 1 green garter 1 blue garter Yellow round hose Parti-color doublet Torn ruff Brown leather boots	4	End IV,2 p. 71	Off SL
IV,1	KATE	Personal panties White corset White tights Dirty petticoat Dirty white dress Muddy slippers Ratty wig	4	End IV,1 p. 69	Off SL

MASTER RUNNING LIST (Form 9-F)

The master running list is a complete listing of duties performed by all members of the costume crew for the running of a production. It can be compiled from the combined charts of costume assignments (see Form 9-G) or may be broken down to create assignment sheets.

Should there be a need for additional assignments during "dress/techs" or the run of the show, the stage manager can tell immediately if he has a crew member available at the necessary time or whether an additional person should be hired. If there is a wardrobe mistress, she will need this list to assign duties to the personnel in her department.

The following is a partial example of Form 9-F indicating how assignments might be recorded:

ASSIGNED TO	PAGE	PLACE	DUTIES TO BE PERFORMED
F. Jacks	2nd Int.	Women's dressing rm	Help Beatrice with change #B-1
		SR change booth	Preset Beatrice, Hero, Margaret, & Ursula's masks
W. Harper	2nd Int.	Men's dressing rm	Be available for any help or repairs the actors may need

COSTUME ASSIGNMENTS (Form 9-G)

The stage manager should be sure he has a complete and separate listing of the duties assigned each member of the wardrobe department. This guarantees that the show can continue should a dresser lose his copy, a replacement crew member join the company, etc. A missing dresser on a fast change or a last minute rush to remember everything one particular person is responsible for can be very upsetting for the cast and affect the performance. By having a copy of each person's assignments, the stage manager can safeguard against such mishaps.

The following example illustrates how Form 9-G might be used to record the assignments for a crew member:

ACT & SCENE	PAGE	PLACE	CUE TO GO TO PLACE	CUE TO START	DUTIES TO BE PERFORMED
I,1	6	SL	JOHN: "All right, knock it off!"	Dr. Lukas exits	FAST CHANGE (15 seconds) OFF: Suit jacket Shoes ON: Smoking jacket Slippers

Some useful abbreviations for this form might be: CH—Change, DR—Dressing Room, and PS—Preset.

COSTUME MEASUREMENT CHART (Form 9-H)

The compilation and maintenance of costume measurement charts is usually the responsibility of the wardrobe department. It is sometimes useful for the stage manager to have a copy of this information, however, since it can be helpful in casting a replacement and determining if the replacement can use the existing costume. In a touring company it may be necessary to make adjustments on a costume for an emergency replacement during the travel time. Since it is extremely difficult to fit an actor on a moving bus or plane, the best thing is to work from the measurement chart.

It is advisable to keep one sheet for men and a second for women. The blank boxes at the top of the chart on Form 9-H can be used to enter the actors' names, thus forming a grid that will allow for eleven actors' measurements to be recorded on one sheet of paper.

COSTUME REPAIR SHEET (Form 9-I)

Although requests for costume repairs are usually made to the wardrobe supervisor, it is a good idea to provide a sheet for the actors to record their requests. Costume repair sheets are often placed on the back of dressing room doors.

The following is an example of an entry for requested costume repair:

NAME	DATE	COSTUME PIECE	DESCRIPTION OF REPAIR
P. Alzado	6/19/82	Blue suit jacket	Button missing/I put it in the jacket pocket

FORM 9–A

COSTUME DESCRIPTION

Page _____ of _____

Act & Scene _____

# of Costume _____

ACTOR _____ PRODUCTION _____ CHARACTER _____ UNDERSTUDY _____ Date _____

SAME AS PREVIOUS COSTUME WITH FOLLOWING CHANGES:

ADDITION OF: REMOVAL OF:

ARTICLE	COLORS	FABRIC	SIZE	HOW FASTEN	POCKETS	NOTES
---	---	---	---	---	---	CLEAN PACK

(List Continued On Next Page)

Undergarments , Tops, Bottoms, Outer Garments, Shoes, Socks, Hats, Accessories, Jewelry, Hairpieces, Costume Props

KEY:

Act & Scene _____

# of Costume _____

COSTUME DESCRIPTION (Cont'd)

Page _____ of _____

Date _____

PRODUCTION _____ CHARACTER _____

ARTICLE	COLORS	FABRIC	SIZE	HOW FASTEN	POCKETS	NOTES	
						CLEAN	PACK

MAKEUP NOTES:

ONSTAGE CHANGES:

CHANGE TO NEXT COSTUME: When Made _____ Where Made _____ Dresser Needed _____

# of Pages to Next Entrance _____ Approximate Amount of Time _____

ADDITIONAL NOTES:

FORM 9–B

MASTER PRESET/COSTUME PIECES

PRODUCTION _____

WHEN	WHERE	SET BY	FOR/CHARACTER	PIECES	NOTES

FORM 9-C

MASTER COSTUME CHANGE PLOT

PRODUCTION _____

#	WHEN	WHERE	DRESSER/ CHARACTER	OFF	ON	AMOUNT OF TIME

NOTES:

KEY:

FORM 9–D

MASTER COSTUME PLOT

PRODUCTION _____

ACT & SCENE	CHARACTER	COSTUME	CHANGE			NOTES
			#	WHEN	WHERE	

NOTE: For More Detail See - "Costume Description" and "Master Change Plot"

KEY:

FORM 9–E

ACT _____   MASTER COSTUME PLOT   Page _____ of_____

SCENE _____   Date _____

PRODUCTION_____

CHARACTER	DESCRIPTION	NEXT CHANGE

KEY:

FORM 9–F

Act ____ Scene ____

MASTER COSTUME RUNNING LIST

PRODUCTION ____

Page ____ of ____
Date ____

ASSIGNED TO	PAGE	PLACE	DUTIES TO BE PERFORMED

KEY:

FORM 9–G

COSTUME ASSIGNMENTS

PRODUCTION _____

Page ___ of ___
Date ___

ACT & SCENE	PAGE	PLACE	CUE TO GO TO PLACE	CUE TO START	DUTIES TO BE PERFORMED

KEY:

FORM 9–H

COSTUME MEASUREMENT CHART

Page _____ of _____

Date _____

_____

PRODUCTION_____

CHEST										
WAIST										
HIPS										
WRIST										
UNDER ARM										
OUTSIDE ARM										
SHOULDERS (F)										
SHOULDERS (B)										
NAPE/FLOOR										
NAPE/WAIST										
SIDE WAIST/ KNEE										
WAIST/ANKLE										
WAIST/FLOOR										
INSEAM										
SHIRT										
SHOES										
HAIR										
EYES										

FORM 9–I

COSTUME REPAIR SHEET

NAME	DATE	COSTUME PIECE	DESCRIPTION OF REPAIR

CHAPTER 10

Lighting

Stage managers are frequently responsible for the lighting of a production. This chapter will provide forms useful for that assignment. Whether or not the stage manager does the actual lighting himself, he should be sure he has copies of all plots, charts, cue sheets, and other information pertaining to the lighting of the show.

DESCRIPTION & PLACEMENT OF CUES (Form 10-A)

This form has been designed to accommodate information pertaining to lighting cues—where they occur in the performance, the page in the script on which the cue can be located, the actual cue, a description of the lighting change or effect, special equipment needed to accomplish the effect, and a rough estimate of the time needed to complete the change.

It is a working form for use during rehearsals. Before technical rehearsals begin the lighting designer and director will designate specific lighting cues, and the stage manager will mark them in the prompt script. The stage manager should maintain a second complete copy of the prompt script and an additional list of all lighting cues as an added safeguard.

The second vital function of this form is to record a description of each lighting effect or change. It is important that descriptions be complete since the cue sheets for running the show contain the technical information needed to accomplish the lighting effect or change.

The following example illustrates the use of Form 10-A:

ACT & SCENE	CUE #	PAGE	CUE	DESCRIPTION & NOTES	COUN
I,1	Preset	---	35 minutes	Garden Exterior, 9 PM on a clear October night. Stars shining brightly. Arbor silhouetted against the wall. Leaf effect created by moonlight shining through the trees. Dim light burning in the window of the house.	NA

KEY: NA--Not Applicable

This information is extremely valuable for touring companies where frequent adjustments have to be made in the lighting, for checking the consistency of lighting effects in various productions, and for launching a second company of the production.

DESCRIPTION AND PLACEMENT OF SPOT CUES (Form 10–B)

Follow spot cues are frequently taken automatically by the "front man." This means that his description sheet should contain enough information to double as a cue sheet.

An abbreviated example of Form 10–B follows:

UE #	ACT & SCENE	PAGE	CUE	DESCRIPTION	INTENSITY	IRIS	COLOR
1	I,1	4	WARN: Phone rings CUE: Sam x CS	PU Sam as he crosses CS FOLLOW throughout song BO with lights #15	Full	Head	NC

KEY: BO--Black Out, NC--No Color, PU--Pick Up

AREA INFORMATION SHEET (Form 10–C)

A list of information regarding areas used in lighting the show and any "specials" employed should be maintained for each production. This information is especially helpful for touring companies; the stage manager or lighting designer can check quickly if the stage is large enough to accommodate all areas and, if it is not, consolidate them. Also, when the company is not traveling with its own equipment the dimmers assigned to each area vary. Since it is usually easiest to spot mistakes in lighting effects by area, an area listing might be the quickest way to discover which dimmer has the incorrect reading.

It is also helpful to indicate the lighting areas on a 1/4-inch ground plan of the set. By using miniature plans the major changes in each cue can also be represented graphically.

Note: the remaining forms in this chapter assume some knowledge of lighting instruments and lighting control equipment. If the reader is not acquainted with these technical elements, it is suggested he familiarize himself with this information before attempting to use any of the forms.

INSTRUMENT SCHEDULE (Form 10–D)

A lighting instrument schedule is a chart listing each instrument with pertinent information including: number assigned to the instrument, size and type of instrument, the circuit into which it is plugged, the dimmer which controls it, the physical location of the instrument, its focus and purpose, the type and wattage of the lamp that should be used in it, and the number of the gel color assigned. Additional notes might consist of extra accessories for the instrument, the cut off point for shuttering the beam, or the amount of spill that is permissible.

This schedule can save time and effort correcting a problem with a specific instrument. Should a lamp burn out, for instance, the electrician can check the schedule for the wattage and type of lamp needed to replace it. This saves making a trip to find out what lamp is being used, getting the correct lamp, and returning to the instrument to replace it.

An instrument schedule is most useful for stationary productions where the number of instruments and the position of each are constant. In a touring company where there is constant variation in the plot, it is best to use the hook-up chart in which the instruments are grouped together according to dimmers. (See Form 10–E: Hook-Up Chart.)

Form 10–D is a standard format and should require no explanation for anyone who has experience with stage lighting.

HOOK-UP CHART (Form 10–E)

The lighting hook-up chart is a list of each dimmer with detailed information pertaining to the instruments controlled by it. In addition to the dimmer number, the hook-up chart should contain the following information: instrument and circuit number; physical location in the theatre; type and size of instrument; wattage and type of lamp; focus; and gel or lamp color. It is helpful to include an area for notes to accommodate additional information.

The information contained in this chart is indispensable for lighting the show, maintaining the lighting, and making preshow light checks. When a company is not touring with its own lighting equipment, the stage manager should carry blank copies of this chart to record changes necessitated by the use of different systems. Information recorded for a touring company will often be more generalized than what is needed for a stationary production.

Form 10–E is a standard format for hook-up charts and should be self-explanatory.

PATCH SHEET (Form 10–F)

Although patch sheets are not as essential to lighting plans as plot and hook-up charts, it is sometimes helpful to have a graphic representation of the circuits plugged into each dimmer. The need for this is greatest in rotating repertory companies when the board is continually being modified or changed from one performance to the next and in theatres which permit other groups to use their facilities during the day while they continue at night. A quick check of the patch panel can be made in a few minutes with the aid of a patch sheet.

The following example is used to illustrate how Form 10–F can be used to make a patch sheet:

DIMMER #	1	2	3	4
Circuit #	24	4	16	70
	52	8	27	57
	42	21	6	
	11		39	
SWITCH POSITION	ON	ON	ON	ON

SAMPLE CUE & PRESET SHEETS (Forms 10–G, 10–H, 10–1, & 10–J)

Lighting cue sheets will vary according to the type of equipment being used. Naturally it is not feasible to include a sample of every possible cue sheet; a few representative examples, therefore, have been selected.

A format similar to Form 10–G can be easily used for non-preset systems such as autotransformers:

CUE #	CUE	COUNT	NOTES	DESCRIPTION
6	1↓0 3, 4, 6↓3/ 15↓4	BUMP 3	VISUAL CUE	Lamp on table OUT SR area DOWN

The essential information which should be included on a cue sheet for these systems is: cue number, dimmers used, degree and direction of the intensity change, timing for performing the change, notes pertaining to execution of the cue, and a brief description of the change that will occur onstage.

When the electrician has designed his own cue sheets the stage manager should copy them *exactly* as the electrician has written them. Modifying the cue sheets for the purpose of saving space or making a neater presentation could be damaging to the production if the electrician has to use them in an emergency. The electrician is familiar with his own notation (even if the stage manager is not) and he is the one who needs to use them.

Form 10–H has been designed to accommodate a simple six-dimmer, two-scene preset board. Often two boards of this nature will be connected in order to create two twelve-dimmer presets. In this system the preset panel and switchboard are generally incorporated into one unit which requires only one person to operate it; therefore, it is advisable to record all information on the same sheet. The following example illustrates the way in which two cues might be recorded on form 10-H:

CUE # __8__   COUNT__25__
SCENE__X__

	1	2	3	4	5	6
X	6	0	3	5	9	3
Y						
	7	8	9	10	11	12

CUE # __9__   COUNT__10__
SCENE__Y__

	1	2	3	4	5	6
X						
Y	0	0	4	0	0	0
	7	8	9	10	11	12

For a larger preset board it may be advisable to record the preset readings on one sheet of paper and the control information on another. This is especially useful when more than one person is involved. Form 10-I is an example of a preset schedule designed for a twenty-four dimmer, ten-scene preset board. When the system consists of thirty-dimmer scenes, legal size paper will accommodate the extra six dimmers. The vertical numbers (1-10) indicate the scenes and the horizontal numbers (1-24) represent the dimmers. Dimmer readings for each scene are recorded in the blank boxes. When more than one preset panel is used, the sheets should be clearly marked to indicate the panels to which they correspond.

A master cue sheet for operating the switchboard may be required when the switchboard and preset panels are separate units. A format similar to Form 10-J may be used by the electrician running the switchboard:

CUE #	PRESET # X	Y	FADER	COUNT	NOTES	DESCRIPTION
7		Y7	↓Y	10	Complete by end of music	Playing light UP
8	X8		↑X	25		Night falling

The sample cue sheets included in this book should not be used when they do not meet the needs of the lighting equipment. It is advisable for the stage manager to start his own collection of cue sheets. He may be able to save himself or his electrician a considerable amount of time by taking a supply of his most useful cue sheets when touring with a company that is not traveling with its own equipment. If the cue sheet he needs to run a lighting board in Podunk, Iowa, is in his files in New York City or Los Angeles, the fact that the stage manager has taken the time to make up these notations is of no value whatsoever.

Date _____

DESCRIPTION AND PLACEMENT/LIGHT CUES

PRODUCTION _____

Page ____ of ____

ACT & SCENE	CUE #	PAGE	CUE	DESCRIPTION & NOTES	COUNT

KEY:

FORM 10-B

Date _____

Page ___ of ___

DESCRIPTION AND PLACEMENT/SPOT CUES

PRODUCTION _____

CUE #	ACT & SCENE	PAGE	CUE	DESCRIPTION	INTENSITY	IRIS	COLOR

NOTES:

FORM 10-C

AREA INFORMATION SHEET

Date _____   Page _____ of _____

PRODUCTION _____

AREA	DIMMER	COLOR	NOTES

FORM 10–D

PRODUCTION _____

LIGHTING INSTRUMENT SCHEDULE

KEY:

#	SIZE & TYPE INSTRUMENT	DIMMER #	CIRCUIT #	LOCATION	FOCUS/ PURPOSE	LAMP	COLOR	NOTES

FORM 10–E

Date _____

PRODUCTION _____

Page _____ of _____

DIMMER #	LOCATION	CIRCUIT #	INST. #	TYPE	WATTAGE	FOCUS	COLOR	NOTES

FORM 10–F

PRODUCTION _____

PATCH SHEET

FORM 10-G

Act _____ Scene _____

City & State _____
Designer _____

PRODUCTION _____

Theatre _____
Electrician _____

Page _____ of _____

CUE #	CUE	COUNT	NOTES	DESCRIPTION

FORM 10–H

Act_____ Scene_____ **LIGHTING CUE SHEET** Page_____ of_____
Date_____

PRODUCTION_____

City & State _____ Theatre_____

CUE # _____ COUNT_____
SCENE_____

1	2	3	4	5	6
7	8	9	10	11	12

CUE # _____ COUNT_____
SCENE_____

1	2	3	4	5	6
7	8	9	10	11	12

CUE # _____ COUNT_____
SCENE_____

1	2	3	4	5	6
7	8	9	10	11	12

CUE # _____ COUNT_____
SCENE_____

1	2	3	4	5	6
7	8	9	10	11	12

CUE # _____ COUNT_____
SCENE_____

1	2	3	4	5	6
7	8	9	10	11	12

CUE # _____ COUNT_____
SCENE_____

1	2	3	4	5	6
7	8	9	10	11	12

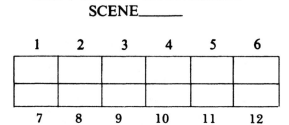

CUE # _____ COUNT_____
SCENE_____

1	2	3	4	5	6
7	8	9	10	11	12

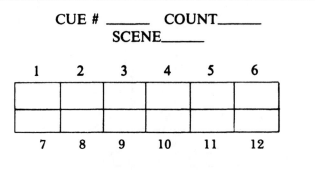

CUE # _____ COUNT_____
SCENE_____

1	2	3	4	5	6
7	8	9	10	11	12

PRESET SCHEDULE

Date _____

PRODUCTION _____

THEATER _____

DESIGNER _____

ELECTRICIAN _____

SHEET NO.

	1	2	3	4	5	6	7	8	9	10	11	12	13	14	15	16	17	18	19	20	21	22	23	24
1																								
2																								
3																								
4																								
5																								
6																								
7																								
8																								
9																								
10																								

FORM 10–J

Act _____ Scene _____   LIGHTING CUE SHEET   Page _____ of _____

Date _____

PRODUCTION _____

City & State _____   Theatre _____

| CUE # | PRESET # | | FADER | COUNT | NOTES | DESCRIPTION |
	X	Y				

CHAPTER 11

Sound

DESCRIPTION & PLACEMENT OF CUES (Form 11-A)

This form was designed to organize the list of sound cues by indicating the cue number, where in the performance the cue occurs, the script page on which it can be located, a description of the sound effect corresponding to the cue, and additional notes such as direction and length of the effect. Please note that in this chapter music is incorporated in the term "sound effect."

This form serves the same purpose for sound as Form 10-A does for lights. The following is a sample entry as it might appear on Form 11-A:

ACT & SCENE	CUE #	PAGE	CUE	DESCRIPTION & NOTES	DIRECTION	LENGTH
I,3	13	25	SAM: "Oh, what difference does it make!" --2 beats-- GO	Door bell	Front door (UR)	1 ring
I,3	14	27	Alice crosses to radio, pauses, turns knob-- GO	"Tennessee Waltz"	Radio	3 min.

LIVE SOUND PLOT (Form 11-B)

Departmentally the performance of live sound effects is the responsibility of the propertymen. The format for Form 11-B can also be incorporated into the running prop list. (See Chapter 8 for notes about the running prop list.) The director may prefer to have the actors assume responsibility for some live effects, such as the ringing of a doorbell. In this instance the production propertyman would be responsible for getting the doorbell, installing it, and checking that it is working for each performance; but he would not have responsibility for executing the cue.

The live sound plot should list all live sound effects in the order of their occurrence during the performance, regardless of who performs them. It should include at least the following information for each cue: cue number or letter; act and scene in which it occurs; script page where the cue is located; name of the person executing the effect; the place where the effect is performed; a description of the effect; the equipment needed and a description of how the effect is accomplished; the order and timing of each phase if the effect has more than one part; and the cues to begin and end the effect.

The following example illustrates how that information might be recorded on Form 11-B:

CUE – __LV 3__   ACT & SCENE __I,2__   PAGE __31__
PERFORMED BY___L. Handley___   WHERE___Off SL___

EQUIPMENT NEEDED: Bell/buzzer box
DESCRIPTION: American telephone ringing
HOW DONE: Push button for bell
TIMING: Ring -- pause -- ring -- pause...
CUE TO START: MARY: "If Jim doesn't call pretty <u>soon</u>" -- GO
CUE TO STOP: Pat picks up receiver -- STOP
NOTES: Approximately 6 rings

SAMPLE SOUND CUE SHEET (Form 11-C)

The primary purpose of this form is to organize the notes the sound technician needs to run the show. The format and information included for recorded sound effects will vary depending on the type of equipment and sound system being used.

The cue sheet might contain the following information: cue number or letter; description of the effect or name of the musical composition; tape and cut where it is located; tape deck to which it has been assigned; speakers that should be used; preset volume and any subsequent timing adjustments that should be made; and the length of the effect or other notes.

Form 11-C is an example of one type of sound cue sheet:

PRESET: Deck__X__ Tape__A__ Cut__1__ Speakers__House__ Deck__Y__ Tape__B__ Cut__1__

NOTES:

IE	TAPE/CUT		DESCRIPTION	DECK	SPEAKERS	PRESET VOLUME	VOLUME ADJUSTMENT	COUNT	NOTES
	A	1	Pre-show music	X	House	0	Fade ↑ 10	10	Fade OUT on 7 count with Sound #2
	B	1	Truck passing	Y	SR	2	Fade ↑ 5	10	Fade OUT immediately
							Fade OUT	7	Also fade cue #1

SOURCES OF RECORDED SOUND (Form 11-D)

The stage manager should see to it that there are duplicates of all sound tapes. This eliminates having to re-record tapes should they be lost or accidentally erased. There may be times when the tape should be reproduced, such as when the original tape has had too much wear or when a second company of the production is going on the road. The stage manager with foresight to record the original sources of his sound effects and music will have saved himself and his sound technician a lot of time—and some money for the producer as well.

Form 11-D is an example of one format that might be used for the sound recorded by one person in a single studio. This list should contain all effects that were recorded, whether they appear as finalized cues in the production or not. It is therefore wise to number them using a system which is noticeably different from the one used for final cues. One possibility is to add the initials of the person who recorded the tapes.

#	DATE RECORDED	DESCRIPTION	SOURCE	NOTES
A-JD	4/9/82	Brahms' Lullaby	Famous Lullabies Delta #349-2	Final cue #3

Notes on this form might consist of adjustments ma e in the original recording (i.e., playing a 33 1/3 rpm record at 45 rpm), the exact portion used (i.e., "coda only"), or the length of the recorded section. Once the cues have been finalized, the cue number assigned to the effect can be entered.

TECHNICAL INFORMATION/RECORDED SOUND (Form 11-E)

The last several decades have seen many modifications and improvements in the types and quality of recorded sounds. These changes have expanded the dimension and use of sound in theatrical productions, but they have also made it necessary to maintain more detailed sound records. No effect can be accurately reproduced unless the playback equipment has features which correspond to the recording equipment.

All relevant technical information pertaining to the recording of the tape should be noted to ensure that the reproduced sound is top quality. This information should be kept in the production book and consulted before calling the recording studio when a problem arises. This list might be able to solve some of these common problems: the tape appears to have been erased (the effect might have been recorded on another track); the tempo is inaccurate (the playback speed may be too fast or too slow); the sound is muffled (the tape was recorded to be played on stereo equipment).

The information that should be recorded will vary with the type of equipment being used. Form 11-E illustrates one format that can be used to make notations on the technical aspects of recording sound tape.

FORM 11-A

DESCRIPTION AND PLACEMENT/SOUND CUES

PRODUCTION _____

ACT & SCENE	CUE #	PAGE	CUE	DESCRIPTION & NOTES	DIRECTION	LENGTH

KEY:

FORM 11-B

Date_____   Page_____ of_____

PRODUCTION_____

CUE#_____   ACT & SCENE_____   PAGE_____

PERFORMED BY_____   WHERE_____

EQUIPMENT NEEDED:
DESCRIPTION:
HOW DONE:
TIMING:
CUE TO START:
CUE TO STOP:
NOTES:

CUE#_____   ACT & SCENE_____   PAGE_____

PERFORMED BY_____   WHERE_____

EQUIPMENT NEEDED:
DESCRIPTION:
HOW DONE:
TIMING:
CUE TO START:
CUE TO STOP:
NOTES:

CUE#_____   ACT & SCENE_____   PAGE_____

PERFORMED BY_____   WHERE_____

EQUIPMENT NEEDED:
DESCRIPTION:
HOW DONE:
TIMING:
CUE TO START:
CUE TO STOP:
NOTES:

FORM 11-C

SOUND CUE SHEET

Act _____ Scene _____

PRODUCTION _____

PRESET: Deck _____ Tape _____ Cut _____ Speakers _____ Deck _____ Tape _____ Cut _____

NOTES:

CUE #	TAPE/CUT	DESCRIPTION	DECK	SPEAKERS	PRESET VOLUME	VOLUME ADJUSTMENT	COUNT	NOTES

FORM 11-D

SOURCES OF RECORDED SOUND

PRODUCTION _____

Recorded By _____   Where Recorded _____

#	DATE RECORDED	DESCRIPTION	SOURCE	NOTES

FORM 11-E

TECHNICAL INFORMATION/RECORDED SOUND

Date _____

PRODUCTION _____

Page ___ of ___

GENERAL NOTES:

#	DESCRIPTION	TRACKS	SPEED	MODE	TYPE OF EQUIPMENT	NOTES

CHAPTER 12

Miscellaneous Tech Forms

This chapter deals with forms that can be used for various technical departments, including those which do not fit under any specific department heading.

MASTER PLOT/BACKSTAGE CUES (Form 12-A)

Some shows contain many live backstage cues. When they involve only one department, it is usually sufficient to make a cue sheet or running list for that department. When there are several different departments and individuals involved it is often advisable to create a master plot listing all live cues in sequence. These tasks may include duties assigned to the propertyman, floor electrician, production assistants, OP stage manager, or stage manager, and might consist of such assignments as live sound effects (props), plugging or unplugging electrical cables on wagons (floor electrician), etc. The stage manager's and OP stage manager's assignment of live cues are usually reserved for such things as cuing actors.

The following example illustrates several live backstage cues and how they might be recorded on Form 12-A:

PERFORMED BY	PAGE/ACT	WHERE	CUE	ASSIGNMENT	NOTES
PROPS T. Lynd	54 Act II	SR	JOE: "By the way, have you spoken with Sally today?"-- GO	Ring telephone	STOP: Mary answers phone
OP SM H. Kerr	56 Act II	SL	Joe pours drink & starts to sofa -- GO	Cue Sally to enter	
LIGHTS J. Richards	60 Act II	SR	Stage in black	Pull plugs & store cables	CODE: Blue

TECHNICAL CREWS (Form 12-B)

Crew information frequently comes in in bits and pieces over a long period of time. It is useful for the stage manager to keep a piece of paper or form in the production book to record and departmentalize crew assignments as he receives them. Form 12-B has been designed for that purpose.

INVENTORY SHEET (Form 12-C)

It is always wise to maintain an inventory sheet of items and equipment belonging to or being used by each department. A format such as that used on Form 12-B can be particularly useful for a long running production. Between the time a show starts its run and the time it closes, the entire staff—including the stage managers—may have changed. When a show closes, the inventory sheet will aid in accounting for all items and seeing to their return. Borrowed and rented items can either be incorporated into the inventory list, or copies of the records of borrowed and rented items (Forms 6-F & 6-G) can simply be attached to the inventory sheets.

An example of the use of Form 12-C follows:

NUMBER & DESCRIPTION	RENTED	BORROWED	STOCK	PURCHASE	RETURN TO	NOTES
1 oriental carpet	X				Eastern Imports 327 Fifth Avenue New York, NY	Insured for the duration of this production only
1 green brocade pouf			X		Stock	

It is wise to use inventory check lists when managing a touring production to ensure that nothing is left behind during strikes and load-outs. These lists may be designed as grids such as Form 3-A or check lists similar to Form 3-B.

THEATER INFORMATION QUESTIONNAIRE (Form 12-D)

The primary use of the theatre information questionnaire is to obtain information about the physical facilities of theatres that might be used by a touring company. This information may determine whether or not a company can book an engagement there and gives the stage manager some indication of what to expect while playing that theatre.

This questionnaire is also useful to record information about the theatre at which the stage manager is employed. It enables him to supply copies of this information to companies that might be using the facilities and to maintain a record for his own files.

The information requested on these sheets will vary depending on the technical needs of the company. For instance, if the company is traveling with their own lighting instruments the stage manager will not have to request information pertaining to that item.

The stage manager may want to include any or all of the following categories in his theatre information questionnaire:

A. Theatre name, address, and phone numbers
B. Contact information for the person in charge of the theatre
C. Seating capacity of the house
D. Stage information
E. Rigging information
F. Notes about curtains, drops, borders, legs, cycs, etc.
G. Loading area and parking facilities
H. Dressing rooms
I. Front of house booth
J. Lighting: Positions, power, switchboard, instruments, etc.
K. Sound: House system, show monitor, intercoms, etc.
L. Unions that have contracts with the theatre
M. Miscellaneous information: Shops, rehearsal space, etc.

It will be easier for the person filling out the questionnaire if the information on these sheets is organized into categories such as those listed above. It is also a good idea to leave space for notes at the end of each section. This permits the person completing the form to give additional information about the items in that category.

The stage manager should always request plans for the stage area, and if he is planning to use the fly system he should request copies of those plans as well. Since many theatres do not have plans of their stage (or only rough sketches), the stage manager must often rely completely on the information from the questionnaire. It is important, therefore, that he ask questions pertaining to anything which might affect the set up or use of the theatre.

Finally, some information may have been omitted or recorded inaccurately. It is always a good idea to update these sheets when playing the theatre and save them for use on future tours.

FORM 12–A

MASTER PLOT/BACKSTAGE CUES

PRODUCTION _____

PERFORMED BY	PAGE/ACT	WHERE	CUE	ASSIGNMENT	NOTES

KEY:

FORM 12-B

TECHNICAL CREWS

Date_____

Page_____ of_____

PRODUCTION_____

SCENERY	PROPS	WARDROBE

ELECTRICS	SOUND	

FORM 12–C

Department ———

PRODUCTION ———

INVENTORY SHEET

Page —— of ——
Date ——

NUMBER & DESCRIPTION	RENTED	BORROWED	STOCK	PURCHASE	RETURN TO	NOTES

FORM 12–D

THEATRE INFORMATION QUESTIONNAIRE

Date _____   Page _____ of _____

Theatre: Person In Charge of Theatre:
Name _____   Name _____
Address _____   Address _____
_____   _____
_____   _____

Backstage Phone _____   Phone _____
Box Office Phone _____   _____
Other Phones _____

Total Seating Capacity_____ # of Balconies_____ # of Boxes_____
Capacity of: Orchestra _____ Mezzanine _____ Balconies _____ Boxes _____

STAGE INFORMATION

Type: Proscenium _____   Thrust _____   Arena _____   3/4 Arena _____
        Other (Specify)_____
Floor: Raked _____   Flat _____   Type of Surface _____
Width: Wall to Wall _____   Proscenium Opening_____ ____
        Center Stage to SR Wall _____   Center Stage to SL Wall _____
        Can proscenium be closed in _____   How_____
Depth: Apron to Back Wall _____   Apron to Curtain Line _____
Height: Stage Floor from House Floor _____   Proscenium _____
        Grid _____
        Can proscenium be closed in _____   How_____
Apron: Shape _____   Width _____   Depth _____
Pit: Shape _____   Location _____
        Is it an elevator _____   Width _____   Depth _____
        Height: Pit Floor to House Floor _____ to Stage Floor _____
        Maximum # of people it will hold _____
        Access to pit _____
Lifts: # _____   Locations & Sizes _____
        _____
Traps: # _____   Locations & Sizes _____
        _____

Describe any obstructions (and their locations) which might cut down on space (i.e., Air Conditioning Ducts, Permanent House Boards, Etc.)

        SR Wing _____
        SL Wing _____
        USC _____
        Overhead _____
        Other (Specify _____
        _____

   Please enclose a plan of your stage
NOTES:

THEATRE INFORMATION QUESTIONNAIRE (Cont'd)

Date _____   Page _____ of _____

Theatre_____

RIGGING

Type: Counterweight _____   Pin-and-Rail _____   Dead-Hung _____

Location of Rail _____   Length of Battens _____

Maximum Weight per Batten _____   Maximum Height of Scenery _____

# of Line Sets _____   # Available for Use _____   # of Electrics _____

Apron to first set of lines _____   Apron to last set of lines _____

Locations of electric battens (from apron) _____

NOTES:

CURTAINS

House Curtain: Tabloid _____   Tab _____   Traverse _____   Other _____

How Controlled _____   Where Controlled _____

Cyc: None _____   Hard _____   Soft _____   Location _____

	#	HEIGHT	WIDTH	LOCATION	COLOR
Curtains					
Drops					
Borders					
Legs					

May the above be moved or removed: Yes ____   No ____

Please enclose plot of your rigging with indications of any permanent flying pieces, curtains, etc.

NOTES:

THEATRE INFORMATION QUESTIONNAIRE (Cont'd)

Date _____   Page _____ of _____

Theatre _____

LOADING AREA

Location: Outside _____ Relationship to Stage _____

Truck Parking: Loading _____

Other Times _____

Door: Width _____ Height _____ Height from Ground _____

Distance from loading door to stage _____

If loading door does not open into the stage area, describe the area between the door and the stage. (Please note smallest opening that must be used):

NOTES:

DRESSING ROOMS

of Dressing Rooms _____ # each can accommodate _____

Locations _____ Distance from Stage Area _____

Toilets _____ Running Water _____ Hot Water _____ Showers ____ Mirrors _____

Mirror Lights _____ Wardrobe Racks ____ Lockers _____ Chairs _____

Are they large enough to accommodate: Wardrobe Trunks _____ Actors' Personal

Trunks _____

NOTES:

MISCELLANEOUS

Best position in theatre for "calling show"_____

Why _____

Shops: Scenic _____ Props _____ Costume _____

May these be used to make repairs for our company _____

Greenroom: Yes _____ No _____ Relationship to Stage _____

Rehearsal Rooms: # available _____ Sizes _____

NOTES:

FRONT OF HOUSE BOOTH

Distance from Stage _____ Uses: "Calling Show" _____ Lighting Control _____

Sound Control _____ Follow Spots _____ Projectors _____

Other (Specify) _____

NOTES:

THEATRE INFORMATION QUESTIONNAIRE (Cont'd)

Date _____   Page _____ of _____

Theatre _____

LIGHTING

Front of House Positions:

	How Many	Distance from Stage	# of Circuits
Balcony Rails			
Booms			
Pipes			
Ceiling Slots			
Booth			

NOTES:

Onstage Positions:

Electric Battens			
Bridge			
Pipes			
Ladders			
Torms			
Booms			
Side Rails			

NOTES:

Grid: Dimensions _____ # of Circuits _____

Main Power: Location _____ Type of Current _____ Total Amps _____

_____ Wire _____ Phase _____ Voltage per hot leg

_____ Wire _____ Phase _____ Voltage per hot leg

Circuits: # in House _____ Amps _____

Onstage _____ Amps _____

in Floor Pockets _____ Amps _____

under Stage _____ Amps _____

THEATRE INFORMATION QUESTIONNAIRE (Cont'd)

Date_____   Page_____ of_____

Theatre_____

LIGHTING (Cont'd)

House Lights: Switch_____ Dimmer_____ Where Operated_____

Switchboard: Type_____

Make _____

Location _____

# of Dimmers_____ Capacity of Each _____

_____

NOTES:

Instruments:

Size & Type	# Available	Lamp	Sufficient Supply of		
			Color Frames	Hardware	Cable

Do you have enough cable to use all instruments available? _____

Jumpers_____ Two-fers_____ Adapters_____

Plugs: 3-Prong Twist Lock_____ 2-Prong Twist Lock_____

Pin Connector_____ Household_____ Other_____

Focusing Needs: "A"-Frame Ladder_____ Movable Scaffold_____

Do electric pipes fly in to stage_____

NOTES:

THEATRE INFORMATION QUESTIONNAIRE (Cont'd)

Date_____   Page_____ of_____

Theatre_____

SOUND

House System: Type_____   Controlled From_____

    # of Decks_____   Speakers_____   Mikes_____   Amplifiers_____

Show Monitor: Greenroom_____   Dressing Rooms_____   Lobby_____

    Other (Specify) _____

P.A. System: Greenroom_____   Dressing Rooms_____   House_____   Lobby_____

    Other (Specify) _____

Intercom: From S.M. to SL_____   SR_____   Switchboard_____   Followspot_____

    Sound_____   Fly Floor_____   Dressing Rooms_____   House Manager_____

    Other (Specify) _____

NOTES:

UNIONS

Name of Unions _____

Positions of Employed Personnel _____

_____

_____

NOTES:

Nearest Electrical Supply House: Distance_____

    Name _____

    Address _____

_____

    Phone _____

ADDITIONAL NOTES:

QUESTIONNAIRE COMPLETED BY:

_____   _____

_____   _____

CHAPTER 13

The Production Book

Once the stage manager starts to gather production notes, plots, cue sheets, etc., he is confronted with the problem of devising a system to organize them. Probably the best way is to use three-ring binders (file folders will work, but they can be easily lost or separated), since pages cannot slip out of order, provided they have been reinforced. Furthermore, materials can be easily labeled and divided, papers can be easily removed or added, and the entire unit is portable.

It would be a waste of energy for the stage manager to carry "dead" information with him to every rehearsal, but it is important to keep copies of this material in case the director or designers should want to refer to it. A simple solution to this problem is maintaining two copies of the production book. This should not be difficult since the stage manager ought to have duplicate copies of all information.

A master production book should be maintained containing all information pertaining to the production from the time the stage manager started working on the show. Due to the amount of information required to maintain complete production records, it is advisable to use three-inch binders. A working production book consisting of only the most recent plans, plots, lists, etc., can be designed for rehearsal purposes. The stage manager may prefer to keep separate notebooks for the prompt script and production notes, depending on the size of the production. The following is a sample listing of some information the stage manager may want to include in the production book:

Actor's Personal Sheets
Cast
   Former Cast Lists
   Understudy Change Plot
Check Lists
Contact Sheets
   Cast
   Company & Staff
   Facilities
   Supplies
Costumes
   Assignment Sheets
   Borrowed Items
   Change Plot
   Costume Plot
   Description Sheets

Dressers' Notes
Hair & Wigs
Inventory
Measurement Charts
Memos
Pictures
Preset Plot
Renderings
Rented Items
Repair Sheets
Running List
Script Notes
Working Notes
Crew Information
Dressing Room Assignments
Expenditures

Long Distance Phone Log
Petty Cash Expenditures
Receipt Envelope
Running Record of Expenditures
Transfer Sheets
Lights
  Area Information
  Cue & Preset Sheets
  Description & Placement of Cues
  Description & Placement/Spot Cues
  Equipment Inventory
  Gels
  Hook-up Chart
  Instrument Schedules
  Memos
  Patch Sheet
  Plot
  Practicals & Onstage Lights
  Script Notes
  Working Notes
Miscellaneous Tech Notes
  Master Plot/Backstage Cues
  OP SM's Cue Sheets
  SM's Cue Sheets
Music
Performance Logs
Production Meetings & Design Conferences
Program Information
  Acknowledgments
  Approval Sheets
  Program Copy
Prompt Script
  Dance Notations
  Fencing Notations
  Key
  Plot Progression
  Publication & Purchase Information
  Script Changes
Props
  Borrowed Items
  Check List
  Elevations
  Furniture Plot
  Inventory
  Memos
  Pictures
  Plot
  Rehearsal Prop Plot
  Renderings
  Rented Items
  Running List
  Script Notes
  Working Notes

Publicity & Reviews
  Flyers & Brochures
  Press Releases
  Production Pictures
  Reviews, Articles, & Clippings
Rehearsal Hall Information
Rehearsal Notes
Reminder Sheets
Report Sheets
  Performance
  Rehearsal
  Rehearsal Time Records
  Touring
Research & History
Running Order
Scene Breakdown
Scenery
  Elevations
  Inventory
  Ground Plans
  Memos
  Pictures
  Preset Plot
  Renderings
  Script Notes
  Shift Assignments
  Shift Assignments (Hanging Elements)
  Shift Plot
  Working Notes
Schedules
  Booking Schedule & Fact Sheet
  Costume Calls
  Daily Rehearsal
  Performance Schedules
  Photo Calls
  Production Timetable
  Rehearsal Time Allotment
  Scheduling Calendar
  Tour Itinerary
Script Assignments
Sound
  Cue sheets
  Description & Placement of Cues
  Equipment Inventory
  Live Sound Plot
  Memos
  Script Notes
  Sources of Recorded Sound
  Technical Information/Recorded Sound
  Working Notes
Special Effects
  Cue Sheets
  Description & Placement of Cues

Memos   Script Notes
Plot   Working Notes
Running List   Staff Memos

DIVIDERS

Naturally this information is useless unless it can be quickly located when needed. Tabbed notebook dividers work extremely well for this purpose. A divider adds another piece of paper to the production book, but it has advantages over putting the tabs on a script page or plot. Tabbing the pages without dividers can result in the destruction of information should the tab rip and can prohibit or complicate the reproduction of information since many types of copying machines cannot accommodate tabbed pages.

The most efficient way to organize the production book is to use a series of divisions and subdivisions. In the above listing of information, the marginal headings would be divisions; the indented headings, subdivisions. Tabbed subdivisions permit further organization within each heading or division. Division dividers can be easily made by using a straight cut manila file folder and cutting it into two 9-by-11-inch sheets. Size 8½-by-11-inch notebook dividers can be purchased at most stationery stores and work well for subdivisions. When the notebook is open, only the division tabs are visible since they extend ½-inch beyond the subdivision tabs. When the division divider is opened the subdivision tabs are revealed.

TABS

Most stationery stores carry packages of 6-inch strips of acetate index tabs which can be cut to the length desired. It is advisable to use a standard length tab throughout the entire production book, as this permits the stage manager to rearrange headings whenever he desires. Furthermore, a 2-inch tab is the most useful size for production books, and pretabbed dividers usually contain tabs of only 1-inch or 1½-inch lengths. Tabs that are 2-inch can accommodate most headings without having to use abbreviations, and five tabs line up without overlapping on an 11-inch divider. Cutting the bottom of the acetate diagonally, as illustrated below, and inserting a straight cut paper can aid the stage manager in changing the position of headings.

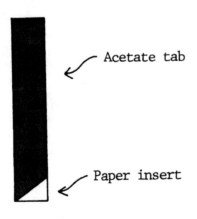

SUMMARY

"Stage Management Forms & Formats" includes 112 working size blank forms. Hopefully many of these will be useful to the stage manager in their present layout. Once again, a reminder that the form should be suited for the purpose; do not try to modify the purpose in order to utilize the form. The stage manager can learn to use some forms, such as the scene breakdown and technical notes from the script, simply by practicing with them in his spare time. Other forms cannot be used until he is in the production situation, in which case it is best to start using new forms gradually.

When designing new forms the two most important things to consider are the purpose the form is meant to serve and the information that is needed to fulfill that purpose. The stage manager should then find the most efficient way of organizing and recording that information. Several tries may be required to get the correct format and optimal allotment of space in each area.

It is recommended that blank copies of frequently used forms be kept in a separate notebook or file. This guarantees they will be readily available for reproduction when needed.

Although compiling and maintaining this information is important to the production, it is certainly not the most important duty of the stage manager. The stage manager should not become bogged down with paperwork and neglect his other duties.